The Craft of the Japanese Sword

Sword tracing (*oshigata*) by Okisato Fujishiro.

The Craft of the Japanese Sword

Leon and Hiroko Kapp
Yoshindo Yoshihara

with photographs by Tom Kishida

KODANSHA INTERNATIONAL
Tokyo • New York • London

PHOTO CREDITS:
All the photographs were taken by Tom Kishida except the following:
Masutaro Azami, 39; Okisato Fujishiro, 56–60, 91, 93, 94, 123–36,
145–52 and color page 15; Shiro Kaname, 5; NBTHK, 36, 38, 64, 66
and color page 10; Otsuka Kogeisha, 1, 3, 4, 17, 18, 20–28, 30, 31;
Yoshikazu Yoshihara, 88–90, 95; Yoshindo Yoshihara, 2, 32, 34, 41,
67, 107, 112, 159–63 and color pages 14 (bottom) and 16.

Names of premodern figures in this book are given in Japanese order,
that is, family name first. All other Japanese names appear in Western
order. For convenience, approximate dimensions and weights are
given in English units. Japanese craftsmen use both metric and traditional Japanese units of measurement.

Distributed in the United States by Kodansha America, Inc., 114 Fifth
Avenue, New York, N.Y. 10011, and in the United Kingdom and con-
tinental Europe by Kodansha Europe Ltd., 95 Aldwych, London
WC2B 4JF. Published by Kodansha International Ltd., 17-14 Otowa
1-chome, Bunkyo-ku, Tokyo 112, and Kodansha America, Inc.
Copyright © 1987 by Kodansha International Ltd. All rights reserved,
Printed in Japan.

First edition, 1987
   95 96 10 9

Library of Congress Cataloging-in-Publication Data

Kapp, Leon, 1943–
   The craft of the Japanese sword.

   Bibliography: p.
   Includes index.
      1. Swords—Japan. I. Kapp, Hiroko, 1943–
II. Yoshihara, Yoshindo, 1943–   III. Title.
U856.J3K37 1987   623.4′41   86–45725
ISBN 0-87011-798-X (U.S.)
ISBN 4-7700-1298-5 (Japan)

Contents

Preface

The authors of this book and the craftsmen it features have known each other for a number of years. The Kapps, because of their interest in Japanese swords, always made an effort to meet sword craftsmen and connoisseurs whenever they were in Japan. In 1979 Leon Kapp's appraisal teacher, Koken Mita, introduced him to a scabbard maker named Kazuyuki Takayama. The next year Takayama brought them to a polisher, Okisato Fujishiro, who asked the Kapps to help with the English-language translation of a sword journal he was publishing. A year and a half after that, in gratitude to the Kapps, Fujishiro presented them with a dagger by a well-known contemporary smith. That evening, everyone went out for dinner, and there the Kapps met the man who had made the dagger, Yoshindo Yoshihara.

Soon after this, as the Kapps and Yoshindo became better acquainted, plans began to develop for a sword exhibition to be held in August 1983 at the College of Marin in Kentfield, California. Several sword craftsmen from Japan—including Yoshindo, Takayama, and a habaki maker, Hiroshi Miyajima—came for the exhibition and spent a month living at the Kapps' home near the college. During this time, usually over much food and drink, everyone remarked on the kind of information available in English about Japanese swords. There were many fine and reliable books, but most were for collectors of antique blades. A few general, historical surveys only mentioned contemporary blades in passing. While several Western metallurgists did attempt to explain how swords are made, much of their information was based on deduction or was second-hand. There was not yet a good English-language source for the contemporary craft and its associated arts.

This book is an attempt to provide such a source. We believe that the craft of the Japanese sword is on the brink of a major creative burst and have here made every attempt to provide a true picture of what actually happens in the workshop of a contemporary sword craftsman. While the description of swordmaking here is necessarily stripped of the quaint romanticism and mystery that is a part of many older, popular works on the subject, including most works in Japanese, it is hoped that in their place readers will discover the aspect of the craft that makes it truly remarkable: how the fierce beauty of the blade is hand-forged using only the most basic elements of fire, metal, and water.

Yoshindo ran the project in Japan, overseeing the illustrations and coordinating the various people involved. Leon and Hiroko Kapp organized the book and provided the text discussions in English (and have taken the liberty of here and there commenting on the work of their coauthor, whose swords they greatly admire). Many others helped, both as contributors to the effort of writing and as suppliers of valuable information and expertise. In particular, we would like to thank Okisato Fujishiro for his photographs and drawings of sword blades; Otsuka Kogeisha for supplying many photographs of antique and modern swords; Takuo Suzuki for his help with the section on *tatara*; Nobuaki Sato for his help with the section on polishing; the Nihon Bijutsu Token Hozon Kyokai (NBTHK) for the *tatara* photographs; Masutaro Azami and Katsuhiko Yamada for their information on steel and assistance in obtaining photographs; and Shigeyoshi Suzuki and Peter Goodman of Kodansha International for their editorial guidance.

LEON AND HIROKO KAPP

YOSHINDO YOSHIHARA

Tamahagane, the traditional Japanese steel used for swordmaking.

Tamahagane is produced by firing iron ore
and charcoal at high temperatures in a *tatara*
smelter.

The raw steel is formed into a block and
heated in the swordsmith's forge.

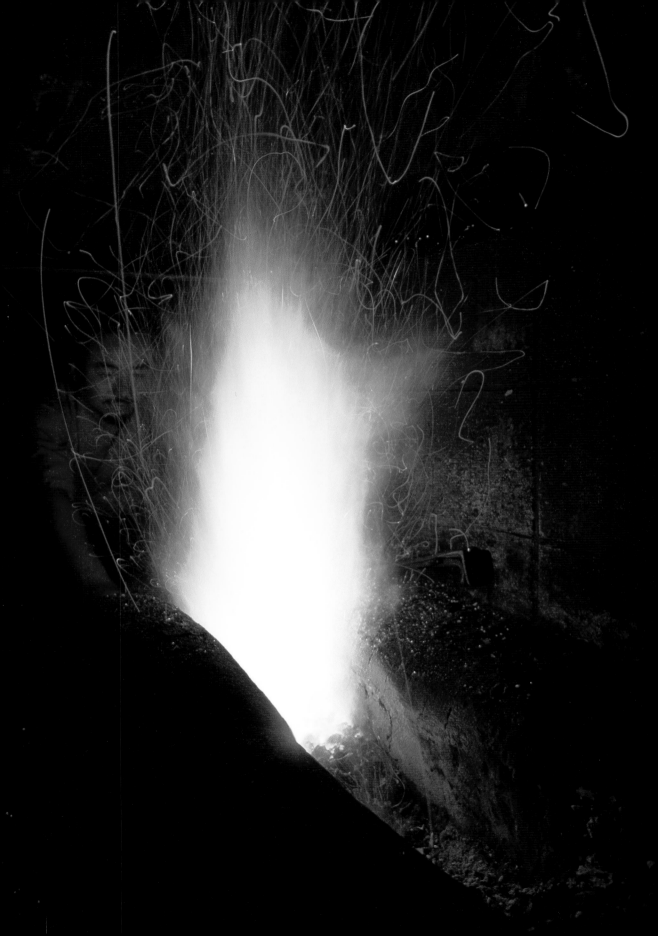

The block of steel is folded a dozen times or more before being shaped into a blade.

Yaki-ire: the blade is covered with clay, heated, and plunged into a trough of water.

Yaki-ire hardens the edge of the blade and produces an array of visual effects on the surface of the steel.

Habaki of one- and two-piece construction covered in gold foil, by Hiroshi Miyajima. The base metal for each is copper, except for the habaki at far left, for which *shakudo*, a gold and copper alloy, is used.

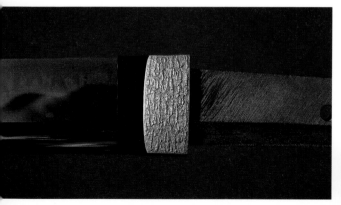

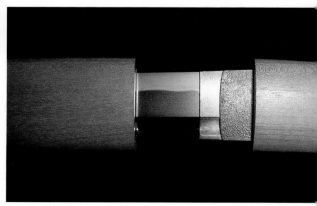

Two swords by Yoshindo Yoshihara, with habaki of two-piece construction by Hiroshi Miyajima and a scabbard by Kazuyuki Takayama. The habaki above uses polished *shakudo* for the inner piece and, on the outer piece, a mottled effect called *koke* ("moss"), created by applying a soft paste of gold and mercury to the filed gold-foil surface. The habaki on the right is covered in gold foil that has been polished smooth on the inner piece and decorated with file marks on the outer piece.

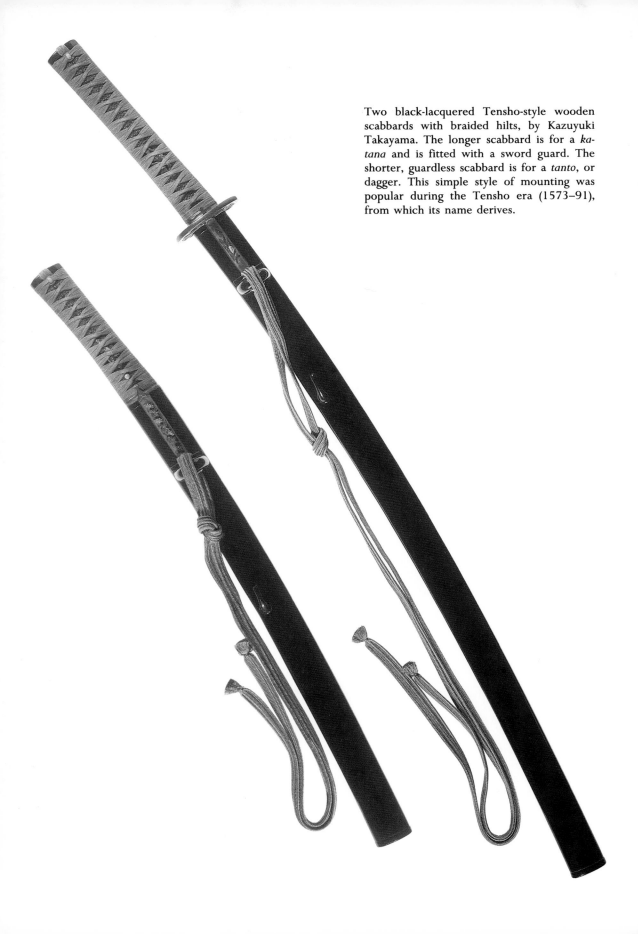

Two black-lacquered Tensho-style wooden scabbards with braided hilts, by Kazuyuki Takayama. The longer scabbard is for a *katana* and is fitted with a sword guard. The shorter, guardless scabbard is for a *tanto*, or dagger. This simple style of mounting was popular during the Tensho era (1573–91), from which its name derives.

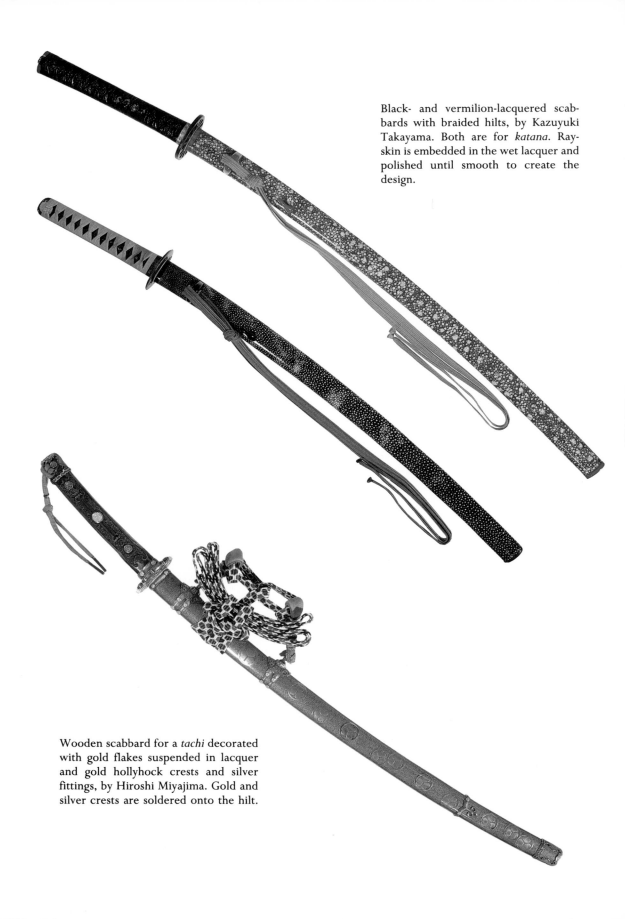

Black- and vermilion-lacquered scabbards with braided hilts, by Kazuyuki Takayama. Both are for *katana*. Ray-skin is embedded in the wet lacquer and polished until smooth to create the design.

Wooden scabbard for a *tachi* decorated with gold flakes suspended in lacquer and gold hollyhock crests and silver fittings, by Hiroshi Miyajima. Gold and silver crests are soldered onto the hilt.

A Craft Reborn

Only forty years ago, it appeared that the ancient craft of the Japanese sword would die out. Under the American Occupation, postwar Japanese were forbidden to manufacture and bear arms. Their swords, many of them valuable heirlooms, were confiscated and destroyed or taken home as souvenirs by the conquering troops. Swordsmiths were forced to seek other work. They quit their forges, and as they did they abandoned generations of accumulated knowledge and expertise. For the first time in history, sword manufacture in Japan ceased, except for a few blades created expressly for public occasions and ritual.

But the craft survived this dark period. In 1953, after the Americans had left Japan, the prohibition against swordmaking was removed. Some members of what was called the "lost generation" of swordsmiths returned to work. At the same time a new generation of craftsmen began their apprenticeships. Thanks to their efforts, the craft of the Japanese sword has emerged in the 1980s as more vital and accomplished than perhaps at any time in the past few hundred years.

This is saying a lot for an art still governed by standards of taste that harken back to the twelfth century. The Japanese swordmaking world is resolutely conservative. As is discussed later in this book, students still have to serve long apprenticeships, living in the homes of their masters and learning the techniques of their craft step by step until they are deemed competent enough to create a finished piece on their own. Designs and decorative motifs are for the most part drawn from an existing body of classical ornaments, all of which have names and are immediately recognizable to connoisseurs. To date, although there are avant-garde kimono designers in Japan, one cannot conceive of such a thing as an avant-garde swordmaker. Even the standard term for swords being made today—*gendaito*, meaning "modern sword"—refers not to their "modernism," only to their contemporaneity.

Limiting the craft's capacity for change and modernization is the unique set of restrictions the Japanese government imposes on it, regulating such things as the number of blades a smith can make each month and the number of years a student must train with a licensed teacher.

One can point out that the Japanese government has no business regulating the work of sword craftsmen. Regulation impedes creativity, inflates prices, and makes it difficult for younger smiths to enter the craft, get established, and earn a living. Yet the governmental restrictions must be seen in a broader cultural context. They reflect the ambivalent feelings most Japanese people have for their war-torn history, as well as legitimate concerns for public order: the sword in Japan has much the same "street justice" stigma as the handgun did in the American West. Also like the gun, the sword is an object around which have grown myth, legend, and numerous works of popular entertainment, as well as the notion that it embodies, for better or worse, something fundamental in the culture.

The sword appears early on in Japanese history. Along with the jewel and the mirror, it is one of the three treasures in the imperial regalia handed down from the Sun Goddess to her grandson to confer upon him the legitimacy and authority of rule. Later, as the cult of the warrior developed in Japan, the sword came to represent the samurai's attitude toward life and action. Successful use of a blade depended not on physical strength but on the perfect coordination of mind and body, on the ability to delay a strike or to fend off an unexpected blow from an enemy. The warrior needed mental calm and resolve. He had to learn how to make his spirit and will flow unobstructedly into the tip of the blade. He could not be overeager in battle, and yet could not fear death or pain. Such an attitude had obvious links to Zen Buddhist meditational techniques. How one handled a sword was thus a measure of spiritual development.

In Edo-period Japan—roughly the seventeenth to the nineteenth century—owning a sword conferred a certain amount of social status. Only samurai, the highest social class, could carry long swords in public. The sword was a visible sign of the samurai's rank: it was the tool necessary to enforce his rule, as well as his means to atone for any grievous error or misjudgment. The sword was also a visible sign of wealth and breeding: decorative sword fittings could themselves be exquisite works of art.

But the worth of a blade in Japan comes from more than its simple material value. A sword is thought to be the repository of its history and of the spirits of past generations of owners. Its present owner is seen merely as the custodian of the blade, and he is obliged to maintain it for future generations to appreciate. The large number of old swords in excellent condition that exist in Japan (blades four or five hundred years old are common) is testimony to the respect the Japanese have for their swords and to the efforts they have made to preserve them.

This mystique of the sword has put an almost occult cast on the craft of sword manufacture in Japan. There are stories of swords that would fight off foes attacking an unconscious master, or that refused to cut a virtuous hero. Swordsmiths were said to have secret knowledge of arcane technologies, and their spirits were said to inhabit the blades they made. There was no shortage of smiths who would exploit these legends for profit—or waste valuable time trying to rediscover forging methods that never existed.

In this regard it is interesting to watch how Japanese people handle swords today. They do so gingerly, with respect and awe, as if the blade were suddenly going to spring to life and slice them or their companions unawares. Sword etiquette is strict in Japan and dictates how the sword is to be held, how it is to be passed from one person to another, what angle it is to be viewed from, where the blade is to be pointed, and so on. These are again the same kind of rules that Westerners apply to handling guns, and they come from the same kind of understanding—that this is an instrument of lethal destructive power.

A case can be made for the contemporary appeal of swords being the result of a new Japanese affluence, self-confidence, and pride. Traditional arts of all kinds are flourishing in Japan today as that country, having at last achieved economic parity with the West, begins reconsidering the ancient roots that many suspect have always been its real source of strength.

A better explanation is that swords today are of a quality rivaling that of the great blades of old. Smiths earlier in this century suffered the lack of good-quality steel and were forced to make utilitarian and usually inferior blades for the military. Today, their sons and grandsons—the postwar generation of craftsmen now coming to maturity and featured in this book—have no technical or material restrictions. Young swordsmiths have access to the best steel forged in traditional Japanese smelters. They do not work for the state but for knowledgeable and demanding connoisseurs. They are affluent. They are scientific. They spend much more time studying and talking to each other about forging techniques, materials, and fire temperatures, all things that were once considered the proprietary secrets of separate schools.

It is in particular the question of what happens next that makes the study of swords so interesting today. As we shall see in an extended discussion below, the consensus among craftsmen and connoisseurs is that a "modern" sword of sorts is indeed emerging, one with a robustness well suited to a dynamic culture like Japan's and that displays a cross-fertilization of styles from different schools and different periods in history.

Such "hybrid" swords will be especially interesting to specialists. Ordinary people will probably detect nothing inherently new in their designs. The fact is that the Japanese sword can exist only within a very narrow range of physical conditions. It must be sharp, easy to hold and to wield, properly curved, forged of good-quality steel, and hardened at its edge but ductile along the body. Any innovations in the physical construction of the Japanese sword were all achieved long long ago.

For most people, then, the appeal of the sword will continue to lie in what has all along made it an object of special fascination. Inazo Nitobe, writing in his book *Bushido: The Soul of Japan* about the cult of the warrior, describes the sword's "cold blade, collecting on its surface the moment it is drawn the vapour of the atmosphere; its immaculate texture, flashing light of bluish hue; its matchless edge, upon which histories and possibilities hang; the curve of its back, uniting exquisite grace with utmost strength." All these aesthetic qualities can only derive from the blade's primary function as a weapon. No wonder they "thrill us," as Nitobe says, "with mixed feelings of power and beauty, of awe and terror."

THE TRADITION

Over a period of fifteen hundred years, the craft of the sword in Japan has developed in response to the sword's evolution as a weapon. As a weapon, the sword had to be efficient, reliable, and practical. The major technological challenge for the Japanese swordsmith here was to develop a series of techniques by which two conflicting qualities of steel—hardness and ductility—could be brought together in a single blade.

The sword had to be hard so that it could take and maintain a sharp cutting edge. But hard steel is brittle and will crack or chip under the stress of a heavy blow. The solution, the Japanese smiths learned, was to wrap a core of soft (that is, low-carbon) steel in a jacket of hard (high-carbon) steel, and then harden only the edge of the blade by heat-treating it.

Virtually all of what we consider the craft of the sword today derives from this basic technique. Beautiful blades are by definition well made. For example, the decorative pattern of the hardened edge, called the *hamon*, serves only an aesthetic purpose. Yet it demonstrates that the smith has indeed hardened the steel, and it intimates the formidable cutting power of the blade. Other attractive features of the metal—its color, texture, and tight welds—similarly testify to the ability of the smith. Appearance was important in olden times, for often a blade could not be truly tested until one's life depended on it.

Koto: Early Swords

The technology that led to the development of the Japanese sword probably originated in China and was brought to Japan by way of Korea. The oldest steel swords found in Japan have been recovered from tombs dating back to around the fourth or fifth century A.D. These blades, called *chokuto*, are straight and have a single cutting edge. A number of them have been partially polished and clearly have hand-forged steel as well as hardened cutting edges. Some straight blades have also been preserved in the Shosoin, a storehouse of artifacts from the eighth century. Scholars believe that many of these old swords were made in China. Some of these are so thin that when held parallel to the ground they bend from their own weight; it seems likely they were ceremonial and were never used as weapons.

By the Heian period (794–1185), when the capital was established in Kyoto, the Japanese had made great progress in improving the imported steelworking techniques. We now see what we can fairly identify as a Japanese sword. The warriors using these blades fought from horseback and so had need for a slashing, rather than thrusting, weapon. In this situation a curved blade was much more effective than a straight one. The blade also had to be long, but light enough to be held in one hand. Swords at this time often had cutting edges of almost 3 feet. Slender and uniformly curved, they tapered strongly from the base of the blade to a very small point, and were worn slung from the waist, edge-side down.

The complex hamon that developed in this period became much broader than in the previous era. *Ashi* appear, narrow, almost invisible strips of soft steel in the area of the hardened edge that help limit the extent of damage should the blade begin to chip. Swords of this period are called *tachi* and are

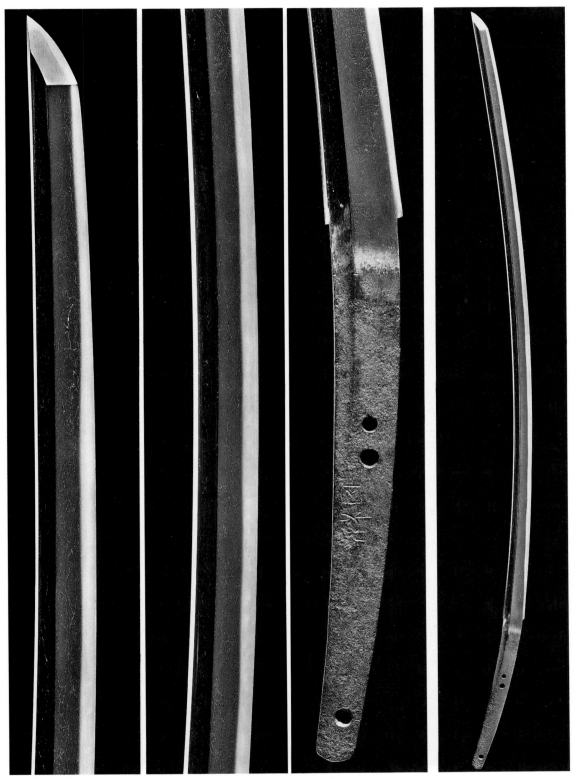

1. *Tachi*, by Kunimitsu (ca. 1300). This sword represents the
Yamashiro school of the Kamakura period. The tang and slender,
graceful shape are unaltered.

2. A samurai using his sword to destroy the demon Shutendoji. From a Muromachi-period illustrated scroll.

representative of the broad pre-seventeenth-century category of antique swords called Koto ("Old Sword") blades.

Not much is known about the smiths at this time. Guilds attached to shrines and temples had the exclusive right to produce swords, and smiths were expected to participate in religious affairs and ceremonies. This reflects the powerful role played by warrior priests, as well as the traditional connection between the swordsmith and worship in Japan. The connection continues to this day, both in the form of purification ceremonies sometimes undertaken before forging and in the manufacture of new swords for the consecration of religious buildings. Most of the carvings found on swords are derived from Buddhist decorative motifs.

In the Kamakura period (1185–1333), Japan was under the rule of a warrior class. For this reason, perhaps, the Kamakura period is often referred to as the golden age of the Japanese sword. Until this time, swords had been made of a single piece of properly forged high-carbon steel. But now smiths learned to insert a soft core of low-carbon steel into the blade. Much of this development was spurred by the retired emperor Gotoba (1180–1239), who is said to have gathered around him the finest smiths of the day and even to have forged blades himself.

The development of swords was strongly influenced by two attempts the Mongols made to invade Japan in the late 1200s. As a result, many smiths turned to making foot-long short swords, or *tanto*, that would be serviceable in hand-to-hand combat. At the same time, *tachi* blades became much wider, thicker, and heavier. The points grew larger, and the area of the hardened edge became broader and thus capable of being repolished many times—a significant technological advance. These *tachi* required two hands to use, reflecting the growing importance of the foot soldier and of close-quarters fighting.

During the Nanbokucho period (1333–92), Japan's imperial throne was claimed by two rival courts. By now the many different swordmaking methods practiced throughout Japan had coalesced into five main traditions or schools, named for the provinces they were located in: the Soshu school at Kamakura; the Bizen school (modern-day Okayama Prefecture); the Yamashiro school in Kyoto; the Yamato school near Nara; and the Mino school (Gifu Prefecture).

These schools are called the Gokaden, the Five Traditions. During this period, and for the next several hundred years, most swords made in Japan were classified as belonging to one of these traditions or to one of its off-shoots. Bizen was the most active school; it was ideally situated for commerce and was near good sources of iron ore. When Bizen's main town of Osafune was wiped out by a flood in 1590—or, as some suggest, by the warlord Hideyoshi—it is said that more than a thousand smithies were destroyed with it.

In the Muromachi period (1392–1568), government returned to Kyoto under the Ashikaga generals. Fighting, however, continued throughout the country, and there was a large demand for swords. Ultimately this led to mass-production and a sharp decline in quality. The intensity of warfare also led to the development of the *uchigatana*, a companion blade that, uniformly curved, could be worn edge-side up at the waist so as to combine drawing and slashing actions in a single stroke. *Uchigatana* were about 24 inches long; they could be used with one hand and were practical for fighting indoors where *tachi* were not.

Shinto: New Swords

An important development around the end of Muromachi times and the beginning of the Momoyama period (1568–1603) was the evolution of the *uchigatana* into a pair of blades that could both be worn at the waist. The larger of the two was called a *katana* and was anywhere from 24 to 30 inches long. Its companion sword, called a *wakizashi*, was about 18 inches long. Wearing two swords became the custom and badge of the samurai and remained so until the practice was abolished in the nineteenth century.

The wide hamon on these blades made them appear much more flashy when compared with the older *tachi*. The steel also appears brighter and more shiny. The texture of the metal surface is different from that of Koto blades as well, possibly owing to the use of different ores and forging methods. These swords are no longer recognizable as having come from one of the five main schools and are sometimes considered a sixth school, called the Shinto ("New Sword") school. At this time, too, the old sword guilds were replaced. Guilds still had the exclusive right to produce swords, but they were now under the control of provincial lords. Individual sword-makers would accompany their armies to the battlefield so as always to be on call.

In the late 1500s the warrior Toyotomi Hideyoshi effectively unified the country to bring the years of bloodshed to an end. In 1588 he issued a decree forbidding farmers throughout the country from owning swords. For swords, this marked the beginning of a great change. From now on, as the right of sword ownership was restricted and the land enjoyed the blessings

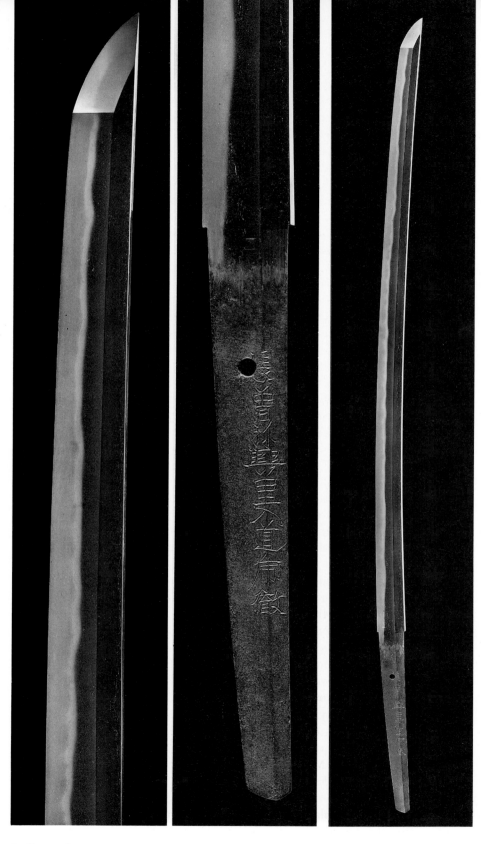

3. *Katana*, by Kotetsu (ca. 1660–70). Note the wide hamon, large point, and very small curvature. The signature is long and quite clear.

of peace, the sword as a weapon would become less important than the sword as an object of decoration or as an indicator of status. Other factors identified by Japanese scholars as influencing the development of Japanese swords at this time are the freighting of high-quality smelted ore throughout the country, which diluted many of the regional styles of manufacture; the introduction of the gun and the resultant change in battle tactics; and the importation of foreign methods and steel by European traders.

The Edo period begins in 1603 with the establishment of the shogunate by Hideyoshi's successor, Tokugawa Ieyasu, and represents a period of peace and determined isolation until the coming of Commodore Perry in 1853 and the restoration of the emperor Meiji fifteen years later. For a while, the Shinto blades of the Edo period were a great improvement over the mass-produced blades turned out during the warring years. But recession, inflation, shortages of iron ore, governmental price regulation, and corruption all made it extremely difficult to maintain the standards of the craft.

The family of Iganokami Kanemichi, who had been appointed "Chief Swordsmith" of all Japan by Ieyasu, contributed greatly to the lapse in standards. The Iganokamis had the right to grant titles or certificates of competence, and this they would do for a fee. Recipients of these titles would then use them to inflate their own fees, thus earning back all of their investment and then some. Some 910 smiths purchased titles from the Iganokami in the Edo period. A record of one such transaction notes that it was paid for with nine *tachi*, one w*akizashi*, a hundred knives (for the use of female servants), and a hefty sum of cash.

Smiths were generally very poor, and many resorted to turning out mediocre blades in great numbers. Tsuda Sukehiro, for example, produced an extraordinary 1,620 blades in twenty-five years (an average of more than 5 per month!). Taikei Naotane's blades are well represented in modern collections but generally make quite inferior weapons; at recent sword tournaments they have cracked and broken. A number of independent smiths, however, refused any compromise in the quality of their work. One of these, Yamaura Kiyomaro, ended up going bankrupt in 1838 and fleeing to the mountains. (He is, however, also known to have forged the signature of the famous smith Kotetsu on his blades to help sell them.) Meanwhile, wealthy lords and samurai were still able to commission finely crafted blades, metal fittings, and sword mountings, many of which form an important part of museum and private collections today.

By the 1780s there were signs of a revival of interest in the great Koto blades of Kamakura times and in the techniques of the Five Traditions. Smiths performed many experiments in forging and welding methods, and also tried out entirely new sword designs. Swords from this period are called Shinshinto ("New New Sword") blades. One of the founders of this movement, Suishinshi Masahide, traveled all over Japan to observe local methods of forging and steelmaking. He is said to have trained over a hundred smiths.

The quality of these blades was mixed. Some Shinshinto swords were very showy with intricate textures to their metal surfaces. Others were very artfully crafted in the old styles. The lot of the smith remained a difficult one, however, and the government remained singularly unconcerned. In 1841,

4. *Katana*, by Kiyomaro (ca. 1840). The sword has a large point, medium curvature, and, compared with the older examples, a wide and healthy shape. The signature, date, and file marks are very clear.

for example, after a period of runaway inflation, the shogunate responded to the smiths'complaints by ordering the price of swords on the market to be lowered.

A greater blow came after the Meiji Restoration when, in 1876, as part of a series of edicts formally abolishing the samurai class, the wearing of swords in public was forbidden. Some scholars have suggested that with this edict the history of the Japanese sword comes to an end. Certainly it was difficult for the smiths, and many were forced to give up their work. But as there was a growing appreciation of the sword as art, fostered in large part by the emperor himself, still some smiths were able to keep working and maintain the tradition of the craft.

Gendaito: Modern Swords

Blades made since Meiji times—called Gendaito ("Modern Swords")—have been greatly influenced by Japan's military adventures. Many blades were mass-produced for officers in the imperial army. Some of these had no hamon at all, and most were produced from foundry steel. They had the shape of traditional swords but none of the hallmarks of a hand-forged blade, neither the hardened edge nor an interesting surface grain pattern. The government today will not register army blades and requires that any ones found be destroyed.

As mentioned above, the Americans' prohibition on the manufacture and possession of swords in Japan lasted for seven years until 1953. Resumption of sword production posed several problems for the Japanese, however. It had to be clear to all that what craftsmen would be making were art objects, not instruments of war. To prevent the large-scale production of cheap weapons with no aesthetic value, the government decided to impose the following constraints on the craft, which are still in effect:

1. Only a licensed swordsmith can make a Japanese sword (any cutting instrument with a blade over 6 inches, a hamon, and a rivet hole in the tang; edged weapons less than 6 inches in length and lacking a rivet hole are considered knives, or *kogatana*, and are not subject to regulation). A license can be obtained only by serving an apprenticeship under a licensed swordsmith for a minimum of five years.
2. A licensed swordsmith can produce a maximum of two long swords (over 2 feet) or three short swords (under 2 feet) per month.
3. All swords must be registered with the police.

The number of swords per month to allow a smith to make was decided by observing the preeminent swordsmith of the day, Akihira Miyairi. A careful and deliberate worker, Miyairi could produce only two good swords a month. Many smiths today can easily produce twice that, and would if they could register and sell them. As this restriction is a burden on the younger smiths, and perhaps even a barrier to attracting new people to the craft, the Ministry of Culture is considering changing this part of the law.

Providing a focus today for the study, promotion, and preservation of Japanese swords is the Nihon Bijutsu Token Hozon Kyokai, the Society for the Preservation of Japanese Art Swords (or NBTHK for short). It was founded in 1960 and is headquartered in Tokyo. The NBTHK performs valuable

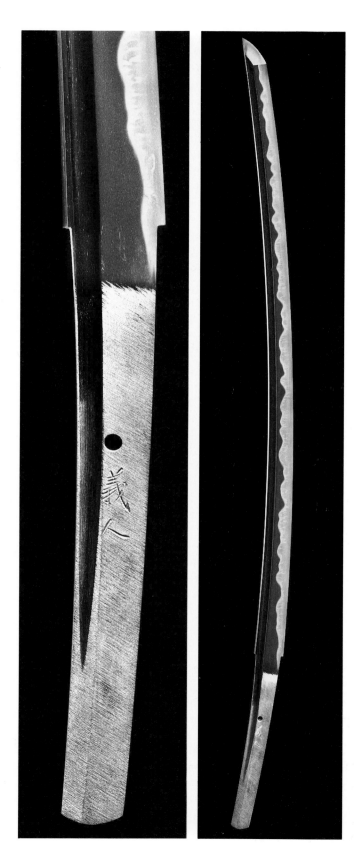

5. *Tachi*, by Yoshindo Yoshihara (b. 1943). The sword is very wide with a large hamon. The tang is white and unrusted, with clear file marks and signature. The large curvature and *choji* hamon are modeled after old Bizen-style blades.

work on the preservation and study of antique swords. It has also done a great deal on behalf of modern sword craftsmen. The NBTHK operates a smelter that produces traditional Japanese sword steel from iron ore, and every year it organizes contests for swordsmiths, polishers, scabbard carvers, and metalworkers. The sword contest is extremely important. In the esoteric world of sword connoisseurship, many collectors do not feel secure unless there is the imprimatur of a national organization attesting to the quality of each smith and his works.

Each smith enters one blade in the contest. The sword is examined twice by a group of fifteen judges consisting of swordsmiths, polishers, appraisers, and collectors: once with its tang and signature covered, and once with them uncovered. The final score is an average of these two appraisals. In the contest of 1986, three hundred smiths entered blades.

All the blades are ranked from first to last. These ratings are considered to reflect the respective levels of the smiths throughout the following year. A smith who wins often enough can be ranked above the contest as *mukansa*. The Ministry of Culture currently recognizes two smiths who were formerly *mukansa*—Sadakazu Gassan and Seiho Sumitani—as living national treasures. Smiths who place among the top ten in the contest form another broad ranking. Contest rank directly translates into earnings: the higher the rank of a smith the more money his work will command. To make a living as a swordsmith, it is necessary to finish in about the top thirty.

One of the NBTHK's most important roles has been in fostering communication between groups of smiths and related craftsmen. This is quite different from olden times, when smiths and their schools would guard their secrets jealously. One old tale tells, for example, of a smith who had his hand chopped off for dipping his finger into the quenching trough of a rival to discover how hot the water was.

But in the years before, during, and immediately after the war, an entire generation of craftsman was lost. Apprenticeships were given up, and elder smiths died out with no one to succeed them. Modern craftsmen thus have had no choice but to turn to each other for help. This and the open spirit of scientific inquiry have a great deal to do with for the increasingly high level of technical accomplishment seen in the Japanese sword today.

STEEL AND THE SWORD

Modern metallurgical science and advanced techniques of industrial smelting and refining enable us to examine Japanese swords in great detail and obtain clues to their manufacture and composition. No one suggests, however, that we can now produce Japanese swords to high aesthetic standards in a laboratory. Japanese sword steel, unlike the modern factory product, is never heated high enough to actually melt and become a homogeneous liquid. A certain amount of nonuniformity in the molecular composition of the metal thus survives the entire process of sword manufacture. As we shall see, it is this nonuniformity that is responsible both for the toughness of the blade and for the complex beauty of its surface texture. The smith is constantly adjusting his techniques as he observes how the steel is responding, and he has in his mind a unique notion of how he wants the blade to turn out. Such an approach to manufacturing is clearly unsuited to a factory environment.

Nevertheless, modern science at least reveals that, contrary to popular belief, Japanese sword manufacture is not alchemy but craft. Metallurgical analysis only confirms the wisdom of decisions made over hundreds of years of trial and error by the smiths in early Japan. Already in the thirteenth century, their swords were at a level of beauty and construction some feel will never be surpassed—without the benefit of gauges, uniform raw materials, or machinery. Production methods were dictated almost entirely by tradition and, except for the introduction of the power hammer into the smithy, still are today.

As the discussion of smelting and forging techniques is necessarily segmented in the chapter on swordmaking, a brief overview of what happens to the steel along the way is presented here.

Steel is a combination of iron and carbon. The mechanical characteristics of a steel depend in part upon the percent of carbon it contains. Iron that contains no carbon would be a poor material for swords because it is too soft to hold an edge. As the carbon content increases, the steel becomes harder. But too much carbon will make the steel brittle, and again unsuitable for a sword.

The iron in steel comes from iron ore. Ore can be in rock form, but for Japanese swords it is most commonly mined as a fine black sand called *satetsu*. Iron in this form is iron oxide (Fe_2O_3). In order to produce steel from the *satetsu*, oxygen must be removed and carbon added. In Japan, this is done in a smelter, called a *tatara*, using charcoal both as the fuel and as the source of carbon.

When the smelter temperature is sufficiently high, the oxygen introduced by the bellows reacts with the carbon present in the charcoal to form carbon monoxide (CO). The iron oxide in the ore then reacts with the carbon monoxide to form pure iron (Fe) and carbon dioxide (CO_2), which escapes as a gas: $Fe_2O_3 + CO \rightarrow 2Fe + CO_2$.

Impurities in the ore (slag) melt at a lower temperature than iron. Bringing the smelter to $1200°C$ results in all of the slag draining off while leaving the iron behind. In some smelters the result is pure iron. In the *tatara*, however, the carbon from charcoal combines with the iron to produce an unhomogeneous mass of steel—called *tamahagane*—that can then be sorted out according to its carbon level and used for swordmaking.

The properties of steel—particularly its hardness and ductility (the extent to which it can be stretched or bent without breaking)—depend on exact carbon-to-iron ratio and on the thermal processing it has received. Different temperatures are associated with different crystal structures, or phases, of the iron and carbon atoms. When steel with a carbon content of 0.7 percent (a typical amount for a Japanese sword) is heated beyond its "critical temperature" of approximately $750°C$, it enters the austenite phase. Austenite has a crystal structure that "opens" to allow the carbon atoms to combine with the iron. When austenite is cooled very suddenly (by quenching in water), its structure changes to another crystalline form called martensite. Martensite "locks in" the carbon atom; as a result it is the hardest form of steel. The more carbon in the steel to begin with, the more of it will be martensite and

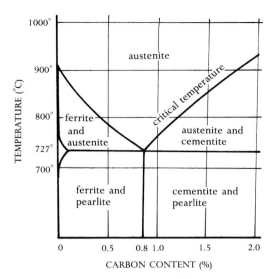

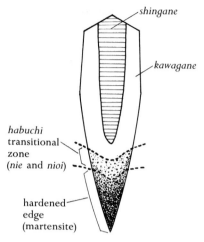

6. Iron-carbon phase diagram. When heated above the critical temperature, sword steel (0.7% carbon) becomes austenite. Cooled slowly, austenite reverts to ferrite and pearlite. Cooled rapidly, it changes to hard martensite. By varying the rate of cooling, the smith produces hard steel at the edge and soft steel along the body of the sword. The critical temperature varies according to carbon content.

7. Cross-section of a sword forged in the *kobuse* style with a core of soft steel (*shingane*) and a jacket of hard steel (*kawagane*).

the harder it will be. As the carbon content goes over 0.8 percent, however, the steel does not become any harder but grows more brittle.

Much of Japanese sword technology and aesthetics derives from an interesting property of steel: if the austenite is not quenched but is allowed to cool slowly, it decomposes (loses its trapped carbon) and becomes a mixture of ferrite (pure iron) and pearlite (a layered mixture of ferrite and another carbon-containing structure called cementite). Pearlite is softer than martensite.

Using precisely controlled heating and quenching techniques, Japanese smiths exploited this property of steel to produce blades with soft pearlite bodies and hard martensite edges. Such a composition made a superior weapon—it could be wielded in battle and maintain its sharp edge without snapping. It is worth emphasizing that the Japanese sword blade is not a laminate but a single piece of steel comprising different crystalline structures. Inside the blade, however, a separate piece of low-carbon steel is used for added toughness.

The zone where the hard steel of the edge intermixes with the soft steel of the body (that is, where the whitish martensite crystals give way to pearlite) shows up on the side of the blade as a visible white line called the *habuchi*. The *habuchi*—depending on the temperature the blade was heated to before quenching—may be narrow or broad, and may contain martensite particles that are either diffuse (called *nioi*), discretely visible (*nie*), or something in between (*konie*). The visible pattern formed by this line is the hamon, and is the most important decorative feature of the sword. A hamon is not visible on a Western blade because usually the entire sword is heat-treated, not just the edge.

Another important feature of the steel derives from its forging. The steel that comes to the swordsmith from the smelter contains numerous impurities. It is also unhomogeneous, with differing carbon contents, some lower and some higher than is optimum for swordmaking. The smith adjusts the carbon content by treating the steel in his forge. He then breaks up the larger carbon crystals and reduces the impurities by heating the steel to 1300°C and hammering and folding it repeatedly.

Different hammering and folding methods produce different textures in the surface of the final steel. These are revealed by polishing the surface—abrading it, actually—with a series of stones of increasing fineness. Forging usually starts with a 5- or 6-pound chunk of steel, and folding it six times reduces it considerably in size and weight. Six or more folds are required to make the steel adequately uniform. But since these would further reduce the amount of metal and not leave enough to make a long sword, the smith about halfway through adds in more blocks of folded steel.

These new blocks give the smith the opportunity to adjust the overall carbon composition of the blade, since not all blocks necessarily have the same carbon level or carbon distribution. They also create distinct layers in the final steel. The higher carbon layers are able to produce more martensite, which can show up as a complex array of effects on the surface of the blade depending on the temperature, the method of quenching, and other factors controlled by the smith.

Among these effects are *inazuma* and *kinsuji*—bright streaks of martensite embedded in the pearlite body of the sword. One important nonmartensitic effect is *utsuri*. This is a wavy, mistlike area of whitish color that appears high on the surface of the blade near the ridgeline. The result of heating the metal to a point in the immediate vicinity of its critical temperature, it is a distinctive feature of Bizen-style blades.

Japanese swords are sometimes likened to the so-called Damascus blades that were in use throughout the Moslem world around the time of the Crusades. Damascus blades were renowned for their durability and formidable cutting edge, as well as for their very ornate damask steel pattern. We do not know precisely how these blades were made, although some scientists claim to have reproduced something very similar to Damascus steel in the laboratory.

Damascus steel appears to be an amalgam of high-carbon steel (1.5 to 2 percent) and low-carbon steel that formed and melted together in a crucible to produce a small block suitable for forging. Forging and working the steel broke up the brittle high-carbon pieces and distributed them throughout the low-carbon body, resulting in the fine damask pattern.

Damascus blades won the awe and respect of the Europeans who had to fight against them. But the Japanese blade is more likely the superior weapon. Japanese steel is certainly more refined, with a more uniform and tighter composition. The core of soft steel in the Japanese blade gives it added toughness. The Japanese blade has a much lower carbon content, and is therefore less brittle. Also, although only the edge of the Japanese blade is hardened, it is hardened all the way through. Damascus blades were probably case-hardened, that is, hardened only near the surface.

APPRAISAL

The value of an old blade depends a great deal on its provenance. Experts—sword appraisers—help determine whether a signed blade or one with an important attribution is genuine or a forgery. If an antique blade is properly polished and in good condition, a knowledgeable appraiser can determine when it was made, the style of workmanship used, the part of Japan it comes from, and, if it is unsigned, the school and sometimes the identity of the smith who made it. If a blade's pedigree is in order, the appraiser will issue its owner a certificate of legitimacy.

Appraisers perform the vital task of establishing meaningful aesthetic standards. Their job is complicated by the fact that while each blade is hand-forged and unique, the practical requirements of a sword are such that important differences between blades tend to be more subtle than obvious and not immediately apparent to the unpracticed eye. A conversation among appraisers can be quite bewildering to the layman, for they use a specialized vocabulary to make ever more precise and necessary distinctions between hamon, shapes, grains, curves, file marks, tang holes, and the like.

Basic appraisal, however—whether the sword is old or new—requires only a simple understanding of what the sword looks like, some idea of how it was made, and a familiarity with the most common types of flaws or defects in the metalwork. At this level, the goal would be to answer the question: "Is the sword complete, properly made, and in good condition?"

It is unlikely that the average person with a more advanced interest in swords will suddenly stumble upon some neglected masterpiece. The swords most people will see in shops and in ordinary collections will be middle-class blades intended as serviceable weapons. These generally are old blades, and often the school they came from and the approximate date of their manufacture can be identified by anyone willing to spend some time studying and examining swords. Most blades, however, will not be distinctive enough to ascertain more than this.

Thus the appraisal challenge for an advanced student of swords is to decide:

1. Is the sword soundly made with no major defects or flaws?
2. Are the shape, the metal, and the hamon good?
3. If there is a problem with the blade, or some damage to it, is it from poor construction or from excessive polishing and wear over the centuries?
4. What school or province produced it?
5. In what period was it made?

One additional problem in examining swords is that steel rusts. Freshly polished swords are far more interesting than rusty, scratched ones. But rusty blades can be repolished and restored. One should always examine the blade and not be distracted by the condition of its polish.

Determining who made the blade (as well as where and when) or whether the signature is good is extremely challenging. It may take an appraiser years of studying swords and signatures and examining authenticated works of various smiths. Reference books on the subject of signatures and styles abound, and controversies over provenance are regularly taken up in specialist journals.

The best appraisers in Japan can answer most of the difficult questions. They must then consider whether a sword deserves to be rated highly, that is, whether it is a distinctly good example of a particular smith's work. A top-rated blade should also have some historical value. Some of its previous owners may be known, or its presentation as a gift or award might be recorded in a historical document belonging to a shrine or a household. And of course a fine sword must be aesthetically pleasing as well as structurally sound.

The standard by which all swords in Japan, new and old, are judged is the body of fine swords that are recognized masterpieces. The exact number of swords extant is unknown, but is estimated at around one million. Of these, 117 have such historical and artistic value that they have been designated as Japanese national treasures. Perhaps a few percent more have generally acknowledged artistic merit. Learning to judge this kind of sword with confidence takes a lifetime of dedication. Few people have the time or the opportunity to attempt this, and most collectors will never even see such a good blade except in a museum.

Nevertheless, a basic knowledge of appraisal techniques considerably enhances one's enjoyment of the historical, structural, and aesthetic properties of Japanese swords. English-language books on the subject are not plentiful but present useful information on styles, signatures, and characteristics of individual schools and smiths. Japanese-language books provide good drawings and examples, and can be used in conjunction with a dictionary of names.

Examining a Sword

Analyzing and describing a sword is made easier by using the same words Japanese appraisers use. Many of these can be translated into English. The words for some important parts and features of the Japanese sword have no proper English equivalent. Some of the terms that will be used in this book are introduced in the accompanying figure. Techniques for looking at the sword—the shape, the hardened edge, and the steel surface—are explained in the photographs.

The polished surface of the blade should never be touched with the fingers but always held with the tang in the fist and the polished surface toward the point resting on a soft cloth or paper.

Shape

Emphasizing the sword's practical function as a weapon is its shape, with its single cutting edge and curvature. Each sword is unique, since it is individually forged from steel stock by hand. But its overall shape (called the *sugata*) will reflect the period in which it was made and the school or group of craftsmen that made it. An important consideration is that the blade be not unwieldy but well balanced and comfortable in the hand. Other aspects of the shape to consider are:

1. Length.

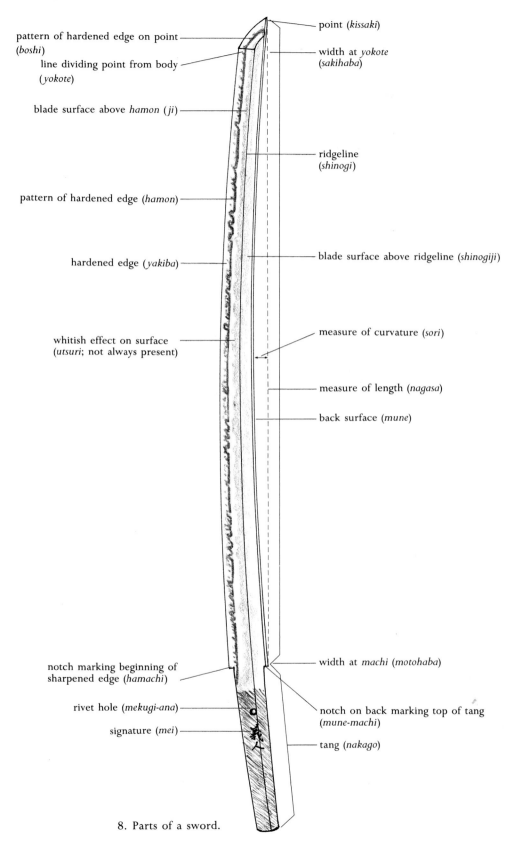

pattern of hardened edge on point (*boshi*)

line dividing point from body (*yokote*)

blade surface above *hamon* (*ji*)

pattern of hardened edge (*hamon*)

hardened edge (*yakiba*)

whitish effect on surface (*utsuri*; not always present)

notch marking beginning of sharpened edge (*hamachi*)

rivet hole (*mekugi-ana*)

signature (*mei*)

point (*kissaki*)

width at *yokote* (*sakihaba*)

ridgeline (*shinogi*)

blade surface above ridgeline (*shinogiji*)

measure of curvature (*sori*)

measure of length (*nagasa*)

back surface (*mune*)

width at *machi* (*motohaba*)

notch on back marking top of tang (*mune-machi*)

tang (*nakago*)

8. Parts of a sword.

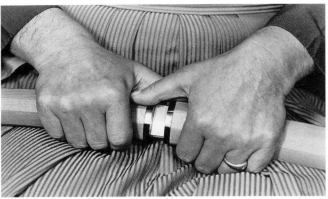

9, 10. The appraiser Koken Mita shows how to examine a sword. To remove the sword, hold the scabbard in one hand and the hilt in your other hand, the thumb of the hand on the scabbard gripping the hilt and vice-versa. Separate the scabbard and hilt by pressing them apart with your opposing thumbs; let your hands act as a brake to prevent the blade from flying out and causing injury. Once the blade is loose, slide it out along its back surface only. Sliding it along the edge or sides may cut the scabbard or scratch the sword.

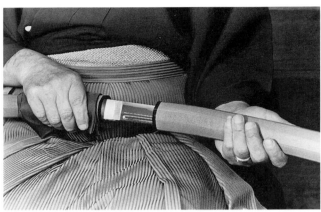

11, 12. Once the blade is out of its scabbard, hold it upright at arm's length to inspect its proportions, curvature, and overall condition. To examine the hamon, aim the blade at a point a few inches below a point light source. The hamon will be seen around the reflection of the light on the blade. *Utsuri*, if it is present on the blade, can also be examined this way.

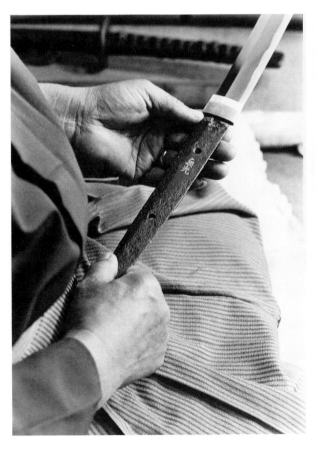

13–15. To examine the steel surface (the *jitetsu*, texture, and color), look directly down at the blade with a light coming from above or behind you. Next examine the point to check the shape and condition of the hardened edge. Finally look at the tang, its shape, the signature (if any), the rust, and the condition of the decorative file marks. Check to see whether the tang has been cut or altered in any way.

2. Thickness.
3. Width of the blade.
4. Size of the point.
5. Size and shape of the tang.
6. Degree of tapering from the base of the blade to the point.
7. Degree of curvature.

Even when each of these components falls into the range typical for a particular school or period, a smith still has considerable leeway when designing his sword. The overall impression of the blade can be graceful, slender, and light, or very strong and massive. As no two swords will have the same shape, each new sword must have its own scabbard custom carved and fitted.

We have already discussed how the Japanese sword changed over time to reflect new fighting conditions. In general, the more strongly curved swords are older (that is, before 1600), while later ones have less curvature. The weight, length, and location of the center of curvature all indicate how the blade was meant to be used and are therefore important clues to its provenance.

Polishing is periodically necessary to remove rust. In olden times it was also done to repair the blade after fighting. A sword that has been polished so often over its lifetime that its shape has been worn down and altered is said to be "tired."

Swords are classified according to size. The blades discussed in this book are primarily *katana*, long swords or full-sized blades that are customarily defined as being more than 24 inches in length. Short swords, called *wakizashi*, are 12 to 24 inches long (sword length, or *nagasa*, does not include the tang). Daggers, called *tanto*, are less than 12 inches long. These smaller blades have changed or evolved over time just like the long swords, and for many of the same reasons.

The Hamon

The most obvious aesthetic element of the sword is the hamon, the pattern of the hardened edge. We have already explained how it shows up as a visible line where martensite and pearlite intermix. It is produced by covering the blade in an insulating clay, heating it to a high temperature, and then quenching it suddenly in water. The pattern of the hardened edge more or less follows the pattern of the clay, since the clay affects the rate of cooling and it is the cooling rate that determines whether the austenitic structure of the heated steel will transform to martensite or pearlite. Often the hamon is polished and whitened (with a *hadori* stone) to make it stand out in relief from the darker surface of the rest of the blade.

The oldest swords have very narrow and straight hamon. For fighting, this type of edge has several disadvantages:

1. The edge, being hardened steel, is brittle and chips easily. A chip could easily go through a narrow hamon, and subsequent polishing would have to grind away much of the rest to make the edge straight again.

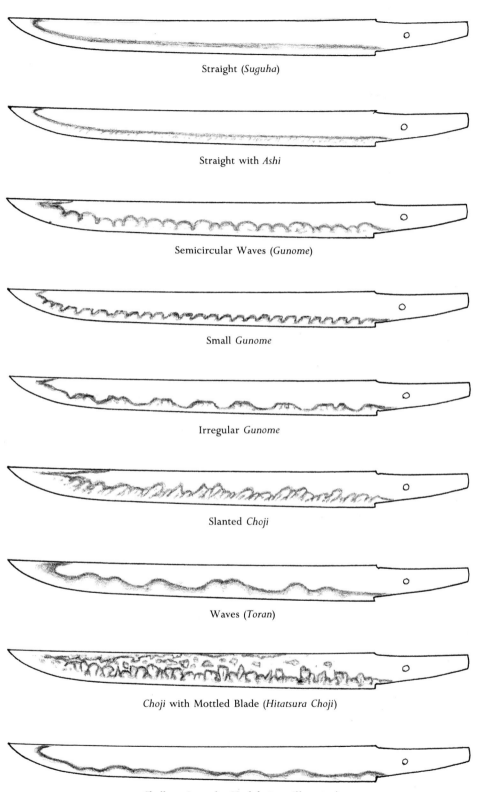

Straight (*Suguha*)

Straight with *Ashi*

Semicircular Waves (*Gunome*)

Small *Gunome*

Irregular *Gunome*

Slanted *Choji*

Waves (*Toran*)

Choji with Mottled Blade (*Hitatsura Choji*)

Shallow, Irregular Undulations (*Ko-notare*)

16. Common hamon.

2. A chip might not extend past the hamon but instead spread laterally across a broad portion of the edge.

In the Heian period, smiths learned to make wider hamon, thus lessening the possibility of a chip going all the way through the hardened edge. They also discovered a new shape for the hamon that would prevent a chip from spreading laterally. This type of hamon is called *gunome*. It resembles a row of teeth, with projections of soft steel going all the way from the border of the hamon to the edge of the blade. These projections are called *ashi*. When the sword is used, any chipping that occurs will have its size limited to the distance between two *ashi*.

As long as *ashi* are present and the hamon is unbroken and wide enough to allow repolishing, any hamon pattern will be equally effective for a good sword. Functionally, then, most hamon are the same, while their designs are under the creative control of the smith, who uses them to complement the shape and match the overall impression of the blade. In many cases particular patterns or variations are associated with specific schools or traditions of swordmaking.

A hamon can appear as a straight line, as a series of arcs, as a zigzag, or as anything in between. It can form an image of a series of clouds or appear like the edge of a saw blade or the roiling froth of a wave. It can be sharp and distinct, or diffuse, like a frayed length of rope.

Steel Quality

The Japanese sword is one of the few arts in steel where the steel's own texture, hardness, and composition—not just its shape—are readily visible and form the most important part of the finished object. Owing to the polishing process, on close inspection of the steel surface of a sword one has the feeling of looking into the body of the blade rather than just along its surface. Unlike factory-produced steel, which tends to be bright and featureless, Japanese sword steel is usually darker in color and has a visible texture. This characteristic color and texture of the steel is called the *jitetsu*. The process of repeatedly folding and hammering the iron to produce a more uniform metal creates a surface pattern in the final steel. This is called the *jihada*.

In the hands of the Japanese craftsman, steel becomes an expressive and lively material. Like the shape of the sword and the hamon, the exact appearance of the steel is under the artistic control of the smith and can be associated with different schools and historical periods. The *jitetsu* in particular will vary greatly with the smith and with the era, and is extremely important in identifying and dating the blade.

Some of the things to look for in the steel are:

1. The *jitetsu*. Koto blades are dark gray, while Shinto and Shinshinto blades tend to be lighter. Bright shiny blades are often made of factory steel. The actual hue of the steel is modified by effects in the metal produced by the particular forging and hardening methods the smith used. On many high-quality old blades from the Kamakura period, which in the opinion of many connoisseurs represent the highest achievement of the craft, the steel often looks like a fine dark-gray velvet.

2. The clarity of the *jihada*. It can be very clear and almost gaudy, or nearly invisible. The pattern of the *jihada* can be wood grain, straight grain, or burl grain, or a combination of these.
3. The soundness of the steel. A fine, tight steel surface results from proper forging. There should be no gaps, separations, or pockets in the steel. The color of the steel can be uniform or can vary and even look rather patchy, depending on how the smith combined the different pieces of steel to build up a large enough bar for a sword.

Some of the visible defects or flaws are the result of forging errors. Occasionally what one person sees as an interesting pattern in an antique sword is nothing but loose or open welds—a sign of poor construction no matter how interesting visually. Other flaws may show up because swords have been polished repeatedly over the centuries and are presently a shadow of their former selves. Sometimes even the core steel in the center of the blade, which is not forged as carefully as the outer steel, is visible on the surface of these "tired" swords.

The Signature and the Tang

Not all swords are signed. A good smith signs only those blades that meet his standards completely. When he does so, he chisels an inscription (*mei*) on the tang. The inscription can be simply his name, but it often includes other information, such as the town and province where he works. If he has a title this can also be included. When a date of manufacture is given, it is usually inscribed on the other side of the tang from the smith's name.

Styles of inscription vary as much as different handwritings of different people. The written characters can appear in blocklike printed styles or more cursive scripts. Other characteristics that help identify the signature are the type of chisel used (wide or thin; this is obvious from the strokes in the metal), the depth of the strokes, and the frequency (how many per inch). Forgeries, where names of famous swordmakers have been inscribed on inferior blades, are all too common. A sword should never be judged by its signature alone.

The tang is never polished or cleaned. When the new blade is completed, a decorative pattern is filed into the tang, and then the inscription is made. Over time, the rust that builds up on the tang becomes an important indicator of the age of the sword. The color of the rust and the clarity of the remaining file marks and the inscription also help to date the sword and authenticate its signature. Cleaning the tang of an old sword can therefore destroy much of its value.

Testing the Blade

In Japan's years of chronic warfare, it was said that you could buy a sword in the morning and be using it that same afternoon. Later, in Edo times, when the country was at peace, there were precious few opportunities to try out a blade. One notable way was to test it on convicted felons, either living bodies or cadavers (as many as three at a time). The results would be duly inscribed on the tang. Many blades by the smith Kotetsu, for example, are so inscribed.

The value of a sword is still said to depend on its cutting ability. Since defects in the forging will more readily show up under stress, testing can be a good way by which younger smiths learn to improve their blades. Some collectors belong to sword-testing clubs and hold regular meetings to try out their blades on soaked bundles of bamboo and straw, or on tatami mats. Usually the swords used in these competitions are relatively inexpensive ones, although a fine sword ought to withstand a few well-placed cuts without serious scratching or damage if it is used properly by an experienced hand. Occasionally swords are tested on unhardened plates of steel. In this case, to prevent nicks, the smith is told to make the cutting edge less acute. Different edge shapes developed in Japan, in fact, as swords changed to cope with different defenses. Narrow and sharp edges were used when enemy armor was made of thick cloth or leather. A thicker, more obtuse edge was used against metal.

About Schools and Styles

Each of the Five Traditions of swordmaking—Soshu, Bizen, Yamashiro, Yamato, and Mino—was located in a different region of Japan. Steel from each of these areas took on a characteristic appearance because of the source of the ore, the type of charcoal used, and the particular forging habits of the resident smiths. Changes in technology and practical needs would cause these regional styles themselves to change over time.

Most of this aspect of sword history is known. As discussed earlier, experienced appraisers can generally recognize a blade as being from a particular school or one of its offshoots in a particular period. For example, Bizen blades from the Muromachi period have a clearly visible wood-grain pattern, a graceful slender shape with a strong curvature, and a hamon in the *gunome* or *choji* ("clove blossom") styles. Bizen blades from this time also have *utsuri*. Other schools similarly have their own styles and features.

Today, most working swordsmiths are producing Bizen-style blades. This is because Bizen blades are what collectors want. Smiths can produce a Bizen-style shape and hamon, and a proper wood-grain pattern, but they find it very difficult to produce the Bizen steel surface. The modern steel just does not have quite the same texture or appearance as that of the older swords, and no one seems to know why. *Utsuri* is extremely difficult to produce and has in fact only recently been rediscovered; smiths have yet to refine their technique. Such differences clearly identify the traditional-style Bizen blade as having been made by a smith in the late twentieth century.

Another important difference between modern and old swords, if both are made in similar styles, is that the new blade will have the complete robust shape given it by the smith. Its hamon will be much wider as well. Some appraisers and collectors of antique swords do not care for such healthy swords, but this may be because they are used to regarding as masterpieces the blades of seven or eight hundred ago whose repeated polishings have made them narrower and softened their lines. Possibly when Koto blades were first forged their shapes were much closer to that of the swords being newly made today. Indeed, the *choji* hamon on some modern blades when polished down to half their width will look the same way some hamon on Koto blades do now.

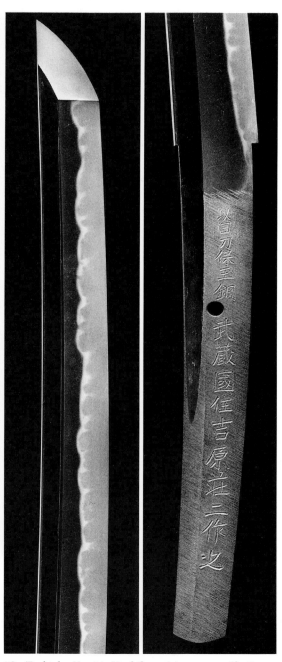

17. *Tachi*, by Mitsutada (ca. 1250), founder of the Bizen Osafune school. The blade has been shortened by cutting off the tang and filing to reposition the *machi*. The lower hole in the tang is original; the upper hole was added later.

18. *Tachi*, by Kuni-ie Yoshihara (given name Shoji; b. 1945). Compare with the Koto *tachi* in the preceding figure and note this modern blade's healthier shape, wider hamon, original and unaltered tang, large *hamachi*, and clear signature.

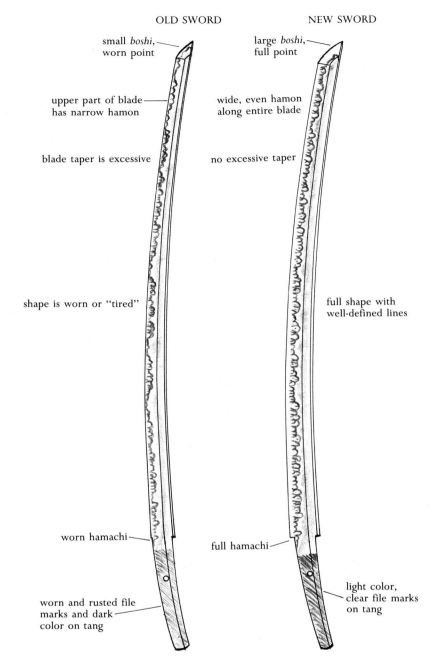

small *boshi*, worn point

large *boshi*, full point

upper part of blade has narrow hamon

wide, even hamon along entire blade

blade taper is excessive

no excessive taper

shape is worn or "tired"

full shape with well-defined lines

worn hamachi

full hamachi

light color, clear file marks on tang

worn and rusted file marks and dark color on tang

19. Common differences between old and new swords.

CONNOISSEURSHIP AND THE MODERN JAPANESE SWORD

The appreciation of fine swords in Japan today is just beginning to include postwar Gendaito. Because the provenance of new blades is seldom at issue, appraisers have never paid them as much attention as they have older blades, and their aesthetic "reputation" has suffered. In fact, for many years these contemporary blades were available to collectors only through the NBTHK show or through personal contact with the swordsmith. Recently an art gallery in Tokyo has begun to offer blades by selected smiths. If this

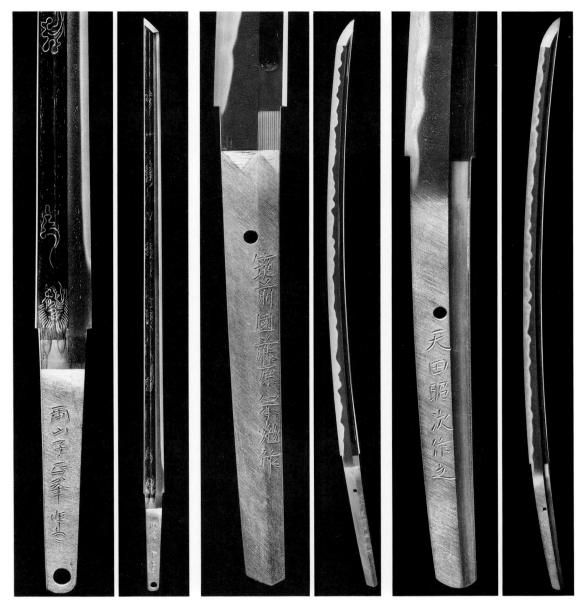

20–22. A variety of modern blades. 20. *Chokuto* ("straight sword"), by Seiho Sumitani (b. 1921). This blade is in the style of a straight blade from the Nara period. Sumitani has been designated a living national treasure. 21. *Katana*, by Tsutomu So (b. 1927). The blade has a medium-sized point, slight curvature, and a very long tang, with intricate decorative file marks. 22. *Katana*, by Akitsugu Amada (b. 1927). The hamon has *kinsuji* and a very diffuse *habuchi*. Amada often works in the Soshu style.

idea catches on it could greatly affect the kinds of blades being produced. Craftsmen might not feel so pressured to take on commissions for traditional blades but could indulge in experiments and place new-style blades on consignment. Contest rank might become less important, making the craft more attractive to newcomers. With this, however, comes the danger of increased commercial crassness: there are already numerous "collectors" in and outside Japan who deal in blades only for profit.

What a true connoisseur enjoys and what serious collectors like to buy depends on their individual tastes. But when discussing swords today, a question that always arises is "How do new swords compare with old ones?" Some collectors like only Koto blades, some prefer Gendaito. It is instructive to talk to some of these people and hear what they have to say.

Koken Mita: Appraiser and Teacher

Koken Mita, now in his sixties, has many students who come to him to study and learn about swords. Ten of his students have gone on to become polishers and scabbard makers. Mita got his first exposure to swords at about the age of five and is the second generation in his family to become a professional sword appraiser. His educational background in swords is conservative and has primarily involved work with older blades.

Mita says there are about two thousand serious appraisers and collectors in Japan today, and probably ten or twenty thousand people who are knowledgeable sword "appreciators." In appraising a blade he says the most important aspects to be able to identify are (1) when it was made and (2) where it was made. In many cases, individual swords are not distinctive enough to tell more than this. Mita believes it would take a casual student about three years to become capable of this level of basic appraisal.

Experience tells Mita that most people like older Bizen blades and that this is why modern smiths tend to work in Bizen styles. Some smiths also work successfully in Soshu styles, but if a smith worked in a Yamato style possibly no one would want to buy the blade. Swordsmiths who wish to earn a living at their craft, he says, should keep this in mind.

The element of the blade that Mita finds most interesting is the color and texture of the steel, the *jitetsu*. He feels that while modern swords are better forged than Shinto swords, they have yet to match their Koto predecessors. Mita notes that there appears to be a change in the quality of the steel around the Koto-Shinto boundary (ca. 1550–1610). He can only specualte about why this is so, but suggests that it may have something to do with the fact that most Shinto smiths were using steel from Shimane and the surrounding provinces whereas the steel used by Koto smiths was made from iron ore mined in different areas all over Japan. There may also have been changes in forging techniques, but these cannot be verified.

Mita believes that modern blades have such good steel because smiths have gone back to the old methods of steel manufacture and are using the traditional Japanese steel called *tamahagane*. Whether it will be as good as Koto steel remains to be seen, however. Part of the beauty of Koto steel, he suggests, might be simply the result of natural aging. Steel expands and contracts in response to temperature changes, and the different layers of steel in the sword will expand and contract at different rates. Over four or eight hundred years, this may actually affect the appearance of the metal. If Mita's idea is correct, four hundred years from now the best modern blades may well have a steel surface equal to that of fine Koto examples.

Okisato Fujishiro: Polisher and Appraiser

Okisato Fujishiro is featured later in this book as a polisher. He has been exposed to swords his entire life, and his family boasts some of the leading appraisers in modern times. Fujishiro, like Mita, also enjoys the older Bizen blades. He doesn't believe that modern swords are necessarily better than high-quality Shinto or Shinshinto blades. He does feel, however, that each era is different and puts a different set of demands on the sword. Modern swords should not be judged by comparison with older swords.

For Fujishiro, the essence of the modern blade is that it is art and is no longer used for fighting. Originality of design is therefore very important, and the blade should reflect something of today's feelings. But even a newfangled blade must be limited by the practical requirements of the sword as a weapon. Shapes may change, for example, but they must be designed to be easy to polish. The characteristics of modern blades that Fujishiro likes are their clean tangs (not rusted from age) and very healthy appearance (not overpolished or worn). Often he knows the artist personally, which of course makes the viewing of a new blade more interesting.

Fujishiro feels strongly that this modern era will have a lasting and dramatic impact on the evolution of the Japanese sword. Even though smiths today have the talent and means to reproduce exact copies of famous blades, they shouldn't. Instead they should develop their own style. Only in this way will they create a solid legacy for future development.

Tadatsugu Shimizu: Swordsmith and Collector

Tadatsugu Shimizu, now in his sixties, trained when he was young in the martial arts, particularly in *iai-jutsu*, or the art of swordsmanship. When he was in his forties and serving with the police he wanted a sword and decided he should help make it himself. He sought out Kuni-ie, the grandfather and teacher of Yoshindo Yoshihara. Kuni-ie allowed Shimizu to come to his shop every day to watch and help. Shimizu then became one of Kuni-ie's students and, later, a licensed smith in his own right.

Shimizu is interested in practical swords. They must be weapons first of all, well balanced and comfortable to hold, almost like an extension of one's body. For Shimizu, therefore, length, weight, and curvature are the most important aspects of the blade.

He especially likes modern swords, because only these can be made to fit his own physical specifications. He admires the beauty of their steel and hamon, and says they are as good as Koto blades. He likes the fact that modern blades are always clean and healthy, with no flaws or overpolishing. Unlike older blades, he says, modern blades don't need appraisers but can speak for themselves. Modern smiths should not merely reproduce the styles of old blades, but should try harder to define their own styles. Swords are a weapon, an art, and reflect the soul of the Japanese people. It is natural that they continue to change and develop over time as they have in the past.

Judges, however, prefer the old-style blades, and since contest rank is so important smiths generally end up following their guidelines. Shimizu feels that the NBTHK could do more to encourage blades to be made in original styles. Dealers also like old swords better than new ones, because they produce more profits and are better long-term investments. Shimizu laments the fact that people don't simply buy swords to appreciate and enjoy over the course of their lifetimes. In a blind selection, he says, most potential sword buyers would pick a new blade over an old one.

23–25. Three modern *tachi*. 23. By Hirokuni Hiroki (b. 1948). The slender blade has a prominent *jihada* and a straight hamon with *kinsuji*. 24. By Kunihira Kawachi (b. 1941). Note the large Nanbokucho-style point with *gunome* hamon. 25. By Sadakazu Gassan (b. 1907). The engraving on one side of the tang shows a dragon ascending a plum branch. On the other side is an engraving of an ancient type of straight sword called a *ken* and a Sanskrit character (*bonji*). Gassan has been designated a living national treasure.

26–28. Three modern *katana*. 26. By Kuni-ie Yoshihara. This is similar to the *tachi* in figure 5 by Yoshindo Yoshihara, elder brother of the smith, but because it is a *katana* the curvature is not as large. 27. By Yoshindo Yoshihara. This is in the *hirazukuri* style: the blade has a flat surface and lacks both a ridgeline and a well-defined polished point area. The engraving, also by Yoshindo, is a stylized picture of a *ken*. 28. By Moriyoshi Tanikawa (b. 1920). This is a wide blade with an exceptionally large Nanbokucho-style point and *gunome* hamon.

Shimizu notes that over the last five years a robust new style and originality of expression have begun to appear. It has taken swordmakers until now to remaster all the basic skills after the mass-production of military blades earlier in this century and the enforced hiatus and consequent loss of smiths after the war. But in order to work at their art and develop and improve it further, swordsmiths must be given the opportunity to lead a stable life. For the sake of the future of the craft, Shimizu says, swords should be better promoted, and ordinary people should be taught to appreciate them more.

Terutaka Kawabata: NBTHK Executive

Terutaka Kawabata is a collector, publisher, and an executive of the Society for the Preservation of Japanese Art Swords. He has been interested in swords since he was a child. At age ten his grandfather gave him a sword he had purchased in San Francisco. Kawabata admits that most collectors are unenthusiastic about modern swords. Japanese people today enjoy the blessings of modern technology and have created a burgeoning contemporary art scene. But when it comes to their traditional arts and crafts, Kawabata says, most Japanese are resolutely opposed to change.

The NBTHK, according to Kawabata, is also conservative in this regard. Its attitude is suggested by the very name of the organization: it was founded to preserve and protect old swords at a time when no good new ones were being made. There was the same sense of despair over the future of the sword as there must have been in 1876 when the Meiji government banned the wearing of swords in public.

Kawabata feels that today's swords are art and, because they reflect today's mood, need not be judged in the same way as the classic blades of the past. One blade may appear merely as a copy of an older blade to a conservative judge, but others may see its large point, rich surface texture, and robust hamon as a reflection of today's good times and strong economy. The main influences Kawabata sees on modern swords are:

1. The generation gap between pre- and postwar smiths.
2. The money that is available to many Japanese now, making swords an affordable art.
3. The good communication swordmakers have with each other.
4. The widespread support for modern ideas and experimentation, and the influence of high-tech and fashion trends.

Kawabata has even gone so far as to compare blades from different eras in a cutting test. For a week he used three blades to cut bundles of bamboo and straw. The Koto blade from the Muromachi period warped. The Shinto blade chipped. The Gendaito blade by Yoshindo Yoshihara cut well and sustained no damage at all. In Kawabata's opinion, the modern blades are not only fuller and more beautiful than the older blades, but they also make better weapons.

Toward a Modern Style

The general consensus among serious collectors, then, is that Gendaito are as weapons and as art approaching the quality of Japanese swords of old. Forty years after the war, modern swordsmiths have remastered the old skills: the quality of the steel, the shapes of the blades, and the appearance of the hamon are as good as any in the past. Moreover, the best of the modern blades today are being produced by the younger smiths in or approaching their forties who grew up in postwar Japan. These swords as a group are classed as Gendaito but are sometimes called Shinsakuto, the "Newly Made Swords."

The healthy appearance of modern swords and the smiths' inability to reproduce exactly the features of revered antique blades are leading some craftsmen to begin fashioning their own details and combinations within the traditional parameters of the craft. Despite the predominance of the older styles, minor changes are being seen in the geometry of the blade, its curvature and tapering, and the size of the point. In general, swords are getting larger, wider, and more flamboyant when compared with work done earlier in this century.

Smiths are also experimenting a great deal more with their forging methods and steels in order to vary the texture and color (*jitetsu*) and the prominence of the surface pattern (*jihada*) on their blades. While continuing to use traditional hamon patterns, smiths feel free to add or combine elements in nontraditional ways. They might, for example, use *nie* rather than *nioi* in Bizen-style *choji* hamon, or introduce a wispy effect in the metal like *kinsuji*, which is rarely seen in Bizen blades. Smiths might also experiment with the shapes of the *choji* lobes, the length and depth of the *ashi*, and the overall complexity of the design.

Swordsmiths are also making efforts to appeal to segments of the buying public beyond the traditional group of collectors and dealers. Knives, or *kogatana*, display all the important aesthetic characteristics of the longer blades—the hamon and *jitetsu*—but are available at a fraction of the cost. They do not have to be registered and are a popular item at department-store sword exhibitions. Also inexpensive, and particularly popular among women, are *tosu*, small utilitarian blades modeled after those found in the eighth-century Shosoin storehouse in Nara. Their hilts and scabbards provide a large area for design, engraving, and decorative inlay work. No less a figure than living national treasure Seiho Sumitani is selling his *tosu* through a glossy color brochure. *Kogatana* and *tosu* are both examples of how an appreciation for blades and metalwork is continuing to develop among ordinary Japanese.

It must be pointed out, however, that most of the changes in new swords are still very subtle and that more extreme design innovations can only be undertaken by smiths whose abilities have already been recognized by collectors and connoisseurs. Moreover, change is still limited by the practical considerations of the sword, over which there is no dispute: the blade must be capable of being polished, mounted, and sharpened, and it must cut well, even if all it is ever used on is a soaked bundle of bamboo and straw.

Major changes in sword styles have occurred in the past and are the reason we talk about Koto, Shinto, and Shinshinto blades. In the near future, as modern swords continue to define their own style in today's world, some term other than Gendaito or Shinsakuto will surely be adopted to name this exciting new era in the history of the craft.

The Sword

Yoshindo Yoshihara (b. 1943) and his younger brother, Shoji, are the tenth generation in their family to become swordsmiths. Both learned swordmaking from their grandfather Kuni-ie, who was active in the early part of this century and made swords for many prominent Japanese, including the emperor. Yoshindo's father also made swords, but after the war, as part of the "lost generation" of swordsmiths, gave up the craft to concentrate on the management of an ironworks. Yoshindo and Shoji worked together until Shoji set up his own shop in 1975. Yoshindo's son, Yoshikazu, began working with his father this past year, and hopes to become the next-generation swordsmith of the family.

Like many craftsmen in Japan, Yoshindo has his shop right next to his house. This is in densely populated Katsushika Ward in northern Tokyo, an older part of the city left behind in many respects by the newer suburban sprawl to the west. People live at close quarters here, and swordmaking can be very noisy work. Yoshindo and Shoji are currently the only two swordsmiths working inside the Tokyo city limits. In deference to their neighbors they restrict their hammering and folding of steel to the hours between nine and five on weekdays.

The Swordsmith and Associated Craftsmen

In the manufacture of an art sword, it is generally the swordsmith who serves as overall supervisor. It is he who receives the commission from the client and then organizes a team of related craftsmen to help finish the job. Usually what happens is that, after the swordsmith makes the sword and polishes it to an intermediary stage, he gives it to a polisher, who works on the blade a bit more to bring out the hamon. The polisher next gives the blade to a habaki maker, who, when he is done, passes it on to yet another craftsman, the scabbard maker. After being fully fitted, the sword now returns to the polisher for a complete polishing. Finally, it returns to the swordsmith, who inspects the blade, signs it, and delivers it to its new owner. Throughout this process, many artistic decisions are left unstated, since the craftsmen are generally familiar with each other's work and know what is expected of them.

All of the craftsmen introduced in this book work directly with Yoshindo and, like him, are part of the new generation of sword craftsmen that has matured in Japan since the end of World War II. The scabbard maker, Kazuyuki Takayama, has known Yoshindo for about twenty years and has been making scabbards for Yoshindo's swords from the very beginning of their careers.

Polishing a new sword takes considerable time, from one to two weeks. The better-known polishers are in great demand and have long waiting lists for their work. Most of Yoshindo's polishing is done by Okisato Fujishiro, Takushi Sasaki, and Nobuaki Sato, all of whom live in Tokyo. Fujishiro, according to Yoshindo, may be the only polisher in Japan studying swords in a scientific manner; he is also an expert photographer of the details of sword steel. Yoshindo especially likes Fujishiro's work because he can produce a very clear and bright hamon and metal surface. Yoshindo will often specify what style of polishing to use, the strength of the *jihada*, the brightness of the hamon, and other features of the blade. When Fujishiro and the other polishers are all busy, Yoshindo may hire one of Fujishiro's several students.

For habaki, the wedgelike collars that hold the sword in the scabbard, Yoshindo turns to silversmiths like Nobuo Asai and Hiroshi Miyajima. Yoshindo had worked for several years with Miyajima's father, and started giving his son jobs after he set up his own shop. Yoshindo admires Miyajima's work for its fit, shape, and finish. He will indicate what style and materials to use, but otherwise leaves the final details of decorative filing and color up to Miyajima.

Training New Smiths

In Japan there is still only one way to learn the art of sword manufacture, and that is to apprentice yourself to an accomplished swordsmith. This is true as well for polishing, habaki making, and scabbard carving, just as it is true for many traditional crafts in Japan, from Kabuki to garden design. All these crafts have had to make some concession to Japan's modernization. Young people have educational requirements that must be fulfilled, and perhaps an independent streak that manifests itself earlier than it did a generation ago. But as long as there is an interest in traditional crafts in Japan and widely acknowledged standards of form, quality, and technique, the apprenticeship system is unlikely to disappear. The skills required by the crafts are simply too demanding to be learned casually and without total dedication.

Students who wish to apprentice with Yoshindo first pay him a visit and talk to him. Some are as young as sixteen or seventeen; a few are in their thirties. Yoshindo alone decides whether or not to accept them. Background and education are not as important as what Yoshindo perceives to be their dedication, stamina, and talent.

The decision about apprenticeship is not taken lightly by either party. Students Yoshindo accepts must live with him as a part of his household. Over the course of several years they learn all the basic skills of swordmaking. In return they receive room and board, plus a small stipend (about

¥50,000, or $300 per month). For this they work and learn as Yoshindo's assistant six days a week.

The student's first task is to cut the charcoal that will keep the forge burning. After that, he learns to flatten and break up the pieces of unforged steel, or *tamahagane*, from which the sword will be made. Next come elementary forging techniques and learning to make and weld handles to hold the steel in the hot coals. Gradually the apprentice learns how to fold and combine different steels, how to make sword blanks, and other basic tasks. Most of these skills are learned in about one year and mastered in three. Learning *yaki-ire*, or hardening the edge by heating and quenching, requires very sophisticated control and may take another two or three years of practice. As a teacher, Yoshindo believes students should move rapidly at their own pace from one stage to the next. This is in contrast to other swordsmiths, who might have their students doing nothing but cut charcoal for the first year, and hammer and forge for the next three.

Thus it is usually five to six years before Yoshindo's students can make their first complete sword from start to finish. Although they can and do make their own small blades (*kogatana*, with cutting edges less than 6 inches long) within two to three years after starting, the government's requirement that all swordmakers serve a five-year apprenticeship before being allowed to register their work makes it rather pointless to begin manufacturing longer swords prematurely. (Yoshindo feels that a very gifted student could get a license in as little as two years if skill was all that mattered.)

29. Yoshindo sometimes uses several assistants when forging a blade.

Their apprenticeship over, and with license in hand, Yoshindo's students can set up as independent swordsmiths. They are now competent craftsmen, but because their output is restricted by the government to two long swords a month it might be ten years or more before they can begin to earn a comfortable living. Helping them establish their reputations along the way is the annual NBTHK contest. It takes seven or eight years of hard work to begin producing contest-quality blades. But there is no other route to acceptance in Japan except through winning some kind of established prize. With only thirty prizes and honors per year, competition is fierce, and doubtless many fine blades and smiths fall by the wayside for reasons having more to do with the politics and economics of the sword world than with competence.

Most collectors in Japan accept the NBTHK's contest rank as an estimate of the smith's work and pay accordingly. The finest new swords are never as valuable as high-quality antique ones, but the price of the work of a living national treasure can at least rival that of a new luxury automobile. Roughly speaking, the blade of a *mukansa*-level smith (that is, a smith ranked above contest level) sells for half of what a living national treasure's blade does. The blade of a smith in the top ten of the contest rankings gets about a quarter of that. Blades of lower-ranked smiths might fetch only a tenth or even less.

The Evolving Tradition

Most of the requirements of what would be considered a "good" sword stem from the sword's traditional role as a fighting weapon. A sword must be practical and functional, and this means it must be well balanced and sharp. Yoshindo has tested his swords for their cutting ability, and he believes that no swordsmith can practice his craft without understanding how the blade is wielded in battle.

Today most new swords are mounted in plain wooden storage scabbards, or *shira-zaya*. Recently, some collectors have been ordering traditional full mountings, or *koshirae*, for their swords. *Koshirae* consist of lacquered wooden scabbards, wrapped and braided handles, sword guards and other decorative metal fittings, and sometimes tiny auxiliary blades and implements. Where a plain wooden scabbard will cost only a few hundred dollars, a full mounting by a top craftsman can easily exceed six thousand dollars. The demand for *koshirae* is partly the result of Japan's affluence but is also an indication of the recognition serious collectors have begun to give the blades being made today.

Koshirae impose certain artistic restrictions on the shape of the blade. For example, a blade that is to fit in a full mounting rather than a plain storage scabbard must have a tang small enough to permit the heftier braided hilt to fit comfortably in the hand. The entire blade must also be made narrower or lighter to offset the weight and proportions of the mounting. The increasing demand for *koshirae* will probably influence swords for the better, for the challenge a mounting brings to a blade inevitably forces the swordsmith to give additional thought and effort to its design. Currently, two or three of Yoshindo's blades receive full mountings every year. The rest are placed in *shira-zaya*.

One development that has given swordsmiths like Yoshindo more design freedom is the decline of the "school" of swordmaking. In the past, different parts of Japan had access to different ores, steels, and charcoals, and local smiths devised forging methods to produce the best swords they could with available materials. With travel and communication between regions restricted, a talented smith with a strong personality could wield strong influence in a limited area. The resulting style and techniques were passed on to students, creating schools of swordmaking distinguished by their forging methods, types of steel, hamon, and so on.

When Yoshindo first became independent he used the methods he had learned from his grandfather Kuni-ie. Today, he can afford the best steel and charcoal; he doesn't have to fight or coddle his materials just to produce a decent blade, as might have been true the past. This has given him an added measure of freedom, and helped him evolve out of the style he learned as a young man. He continues to work in the Bizen tradition, but he has been able to choose his design elements freely, and to create blades that are his own interpretations of that tradition.

Yoshindo and Shoji make an interesting study in this regard. Although they worked together until 1975, today their short-sword styles are markedly different: Shoji's blades are now wide and thin, while Yoshindo's have grown narrower and thicker. Similarly, Yoshindo's and Shoji's students will likely adopt their teachers' styles for a few years after their apprenticeship and then diverge as they become more confident and self-reliant.

Clients also have an influence on the kinds of swords being produced today. About half of Yoshindo's customers specify only the length of the blade and leave everything else up to him. The rest specify almost everything: the type of hamon, the curvature, the length, even the style of blade. Recently an art dealer has been willing to buy most of Yoshindo's blades. Yoshindo prefers selling through a dealer because he doesn't like to argue about prices or worry about having a customer change his mind about what he wants. Selling through a third party also allows him to spend more time on his work.

In many respects Yoshindo is representative of how the sword world in Japan is changing. He is friendly and hospitable, gregarious, opinionated, deliberately provocative, and ready to try almost anything, from model shipbuilding to carpentry to pottery (he has installed a kiln in his house). He can produce just about any hamon he wants as well as any shape of sword, and he is always experimenting with different steel and different designs.

Yoshindo's Shop

The most important feature of a swordsmith's shop is that it be able to contain a very hot fire. The ground must be dry so that there is no evaporative cooling of the coals from below. The building should also be fireproof, which is why most smiths today build their shops out of aluminum and steel. Yoshindo, however, prefers an old-fashioned Japanese design using a tiled roof, wood framing, and heavy beams made out of whole tree trunks. In fifteen years, his shop has been heavily damaged by fire three times, but he keeps rebuilding it the same way.

Yoshindo's shop is a single large room, 25 feet long by 15 feet wide. The

30, 31. Swords by the Yoshihara brothers, Shoji (*left*) and Yoshindo.
Shoji's hamon are uniform and mostly parallel to the edge, while
Yoshindo's are as a rule more dynamic and active.

walls are of mortar, and the ceiling is almost 15 feet above the earthen floor.
Heavy hammering takes place around the forge area, which is about 15 feet
long by 12 feet wide. Yoshindo spends about a quarter of his time here.
Another quarter of his time is used for making charcoal, tempering, and
other shop tasks, while the remaining half is used for finishing work such as
filing and grinding, carving decorative grooves, and completing the tang.
Because finishing work demands a clean, well-lit environment, it is done in
an auxiliary shop away from the forging area, which is always dark and
coated with fine black dust from the charcoal and the hammering.

The forging area is kept dark on purpose to allow the smith to judge ac-
curately the temperature of the steel during forging and during *yaki-ire*. This

32. Yoshindo's shop.

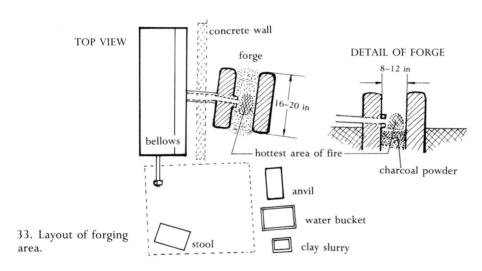

TOP VIEW

concrete wall

forge

DETAIL OF FORGE

8–12 in

16–20 in

bellows

hottest area of fire

charcoal powder

anvil

water bucket

33. Layout of forging area.

stool

clay slurry

is crucial to the manufacturing process, where no scientific instrumentation is used and everything is judged by eye, feel, and experience. Folding and welding, for example, are done at high temperatures (bright yellow) to get a good strong weld. Hammering the blade into shape is done at a slightly lower temperature (bright red to bright orange to yellow): too low (cherry red) could cause the blade to crack, while too high (bright yellow) will soften the steel and make it difficult to control. In Yoshindo's shop there are two small windows, one behind the forge and one over a workbench, and a large window on the north side. During *yaki-ire*, temperature control is so critical that the work is always done after nightfall, the sole light available being that cast by the fiercely glowing blade.

Yoshindo's forge sits directly on the ground and consists of two parallel rows of firebricks about 10 inches apart. The firebrick rows are covered in clay and resemble long, smooth mounds. The smith sits facing one end of the open forge on a low stool, only a few inches off the ground. To his left is a wooden bellows that he pumps with his left hand. The bellows is protected from the heat of the forge by a low concrete wall. A small, 2-inch diameter pipe (tuyère) conducts the air blast from the bellows through the base of the concrete and forge walls and into the central area of the forge, where charcoal is piled and heated. Traditionally the swordsmith would fire up his forge by hammering away at the top of an iron bar until it began to glow from the heat, and then touching the hot iron to a thin piece of cypress wood coated with sulphur. Today, Yoshindo uses matches and newspaper.

To Yoshindo's right as he works is the anvil, positioned to receive steel for hammering directly from the forge. The anvil is a simple block of steel 5 inches thick and 10 inches long, with a flat working surface some 10 inches above the ground. For stability, the base of the anvil is buried 18 inches into the earthen floor.

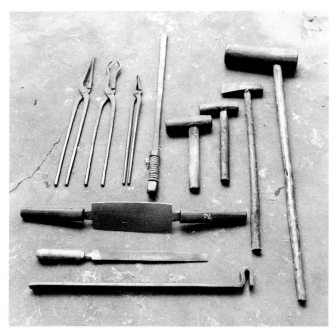

34. Some of Yoshindo's tools. The sledgehammer is used when forging; smaller hand-held hammers are used to shape the blade from the blank, or *sunobe*. Different tongs are used for handling red-hot steel. The hooked tool at the bottom of the photograph is used to straighten a warped or twisted blade. The long bar with the rope handle is welded to the sword steel and used to hold it in the hot forge. Because the bar is not the best quality metal, the part of the sword nearest to it becomes the tang.

35. Yoshindo's power hammer.

Yoshindo uses several different kinds of tongs and hammers for forging. The hammers come in all sizes and weights and are distinguished from their Western counterparts by the way the handle, either a small tree trunk or a branch, is inserted not in the center but near the end of the cylindrical steel head.

The other major piece of equipment in Yoshindo's shop is his power hammer. It is driven by an overhead electric motor and controlled by a foot pedal. Pressure on the pedal controls the rate and force of the hammering, leaving the smith's hands free to hold and move the steel. Yoshindo uses the power hammer for all folding and welding operations up to the shaping of the sword blank. Subsequent forging operations can be done with a small hand-held hammer. The power hammer does the work of three trained assistants. With it, a modern smith can run his shop and produce swords virtually singlehanded.

THE CRAFT

The rest of this chapter describes the making of a *katana*, a long sword with a single hardened edge and an inner core of soft, low-carbon steel. Yoshindo's methods are representative of his craft, but other swordmakers may handle the details or order of the work quite differently. Yoshindo himself will also vary his style and techniques to suit the individual blade and the client. The dimensions and weights given here are therefore average figures that will vary with each sword Yoshindo makes.

The processes described here are also used to make other kinds of bladed weapons in Japan. Daggers and small knives are usually made from a single piece of steel instead of being a composite like the long swords. For more information about steel and the parts of the sword, see the introductory chapter.

Tamahagane: Japanese Steel

Steel is iron that contains carbon: the more carbon, the harder the steel. Most swordsmiths in Japan work with a traditional form of steel called *tamahagane*. This is produced today almost exclusively in a single Japanese-style smelter, called a *tatara*, operated by the NBTHK in Yokota, a small town in Shimane Prefecture, western Honshu. The *tatara*, like other smelters, relies on the propensity of very hot iron to combine with carbon in its vicinity to produce steel. In the *tatara*, it is burning charcoal that supplies the carbon. Although the Japanese *tatara* is very efficient, the *tamahagane* it produces is still fairly crude at the time it reaches the smith, who refines it by forging to reduce the carbon content and to make a more malleable final steel suitable for swordmaking.

Swords can also be made out of electrolytic iron (*denkai-tetsu*), which is 99.99 percent pure iron made from scrap iron in an electric furnace. By processing it in a small home smelter, the smith can add an appropriate amount of carbon to the steel. Similarly, sponge iron (*kangan-tetsu*), produced by removing all oxygen during smelting, is smelted again by the smith with a charcoal fire to obtain high-carbon steel.

Yoshindo's first choice is always *tamahagane*, which he feels is easiest to forge and produces the best steel for swords. There are large differences in the cost of these materials. *Tamahagane* costs about $20 per pound; electrolytic iron costs $3 per pound. Sponge iron costs $65 per *ton*. Since a smith needs 5 or 6 pounds of *tamahagane* to produce a single pound of sword steel, *tamahagane* for just a single blade can end up costing as much as $200.

The NBTHK smelter in Shimane Prefecture has been the responsibility of Takuo Suzuki since the mid-1970s. He travels there about six or seven times a year, often accompanied by Yoshindo, to teach young swordsmiths about the *tatara* and its operation. Suzuki is always tracking down historical references and sites to learn more about how *tatara* smelters were developed and used by ancient metalworkers in Japan.

The *tatara* does not appear to be a Japanese invention. It may have come from Manchuria by way of the Korean peninsula in the sixth or seventh century A.D. By the ninth century, *tatara* were in use throughout Japan, primarily by small groups of steelworkers mining and smelting their own steel for ornaments, tools, and armaments. In the Muromachi period, technological innovations resulted in mass production beginning in selected centers, among them Shimane on the Japan Sea. The Shimane area had long been recognized for its plentiful supply of both charcoal for smelting and high-quality iron sand. By the end of the Edo period, about 80 percent of all Japanese steel was being made there. Shimane steelworkers may have been responsible for two important innovations in smelting technology in the 1400s: the use of drain holes to let the molten slag run off, and the increase

36. Silk scroll painting showing the premodern operation of a *tatara* smelter. The chief is holding the shovel, while his four assistants coordinate the pumping of the bellows. By Nagashio Setsuzan (1774–1833).

in size of the smelter itself. Some old *tatara* sites discovered in the mountains of Shimane Prefecture are still plugged up with huge slabs of smelted steel that presumably had been too large and heavy for workmen to remove.

These Muromachi-style *tatara* operated continuously in Japan throughout the Edo period. They ran primarily during the winter months, when it was cold and when the labor of farmers was available. Gradually production declined, however, and the last such *tatara* shut down in 1925. In 1933, Yasukuni Shrine in Tokyo, which enjoyed close ties with the military and governmental authorities, established its own *tatara* in Shimane to produce *tamahagane* for smiths working at the shrine forges. Operation of the Yasukuni *tatara* ceased in 1944. In 1975 the NBTHK, looking for a source of traditional steel, decided to fire up the Shimane smelter again. Luckily, to help get things underway there were written records from earlier this century, and one of the old operators still lived in the area and was eager to work with the *tatara* again. Today he is one of a dozen men who labor in two twelve-hour shifts each day when the furnace is in use.

Iron ore in Shimane occurs in the form of a black sand called *satetsu*. The product of erosive action in natural iron ore deposits, *satetsu* is frequently found in or near streambeds, mixed in with other silts and sediments. Only about 1 percent of the sand mixture is iron. In Edo times this was removed by running the sand into water channels with ripple bars along the bottom. The heavier iron sand would fall behind the bars as the water carried off the lighter sand. This old method still retains its virtues—it is economical, and produces very clean ore—but concern over pollution and the environmental impact of sediment has caused it to be abandoned. Today, the bulk sand is mined with a bulldozer. The iron ore is then extracted by a magnet and transported to the *tatara* by truck.

Essentially a *tatara* is a trough made of clay, about 5 feet wide, 48 inches tall, and 15 feet long. Its walls are 10 inches thick. The site for the *tatara* is prepared by creating a huge subsurface complex using clay and stone with wooden walls and pilings for drainage and support. The area just beneath the smelter is loaded with charcoal and burned until it is filled with ashes. If built correctly, this underground structure will last for many years and will effectively prevent any residual moisture from evaporating and lowering the temperature of the *tatara* during firing.

Each time before the *tatara* is used, its walls must be built anew out of clay bricks. The clay mixture contains a large amount of sand (silicon oxide), which makes it resistant to fire and melting. Holes in the base of each wall are left for twenty bamboo bellow pipes. Bellows stand on either side of the trough. In olden times they were operated by hand like the bellows in the smithy. In the Edo period the design was modified to allow them to be pumped by continuous foot action, thus increasing their capacity. Today they are driven by electric motors.

One operating cycle of the *tatara* takes five days: one day to build the walls from clay and sand; three days to smelt; and one day to remove the iron. After the walls are up, a small fire is started in the bottom of the trough, and fist-sized pieces of oak and pine charcoal are added continuously for three hours. Then the top of the coals is spread with iron sand, followed immediately by a layer of charcoal. Thirty minutes later more iron sand and char-

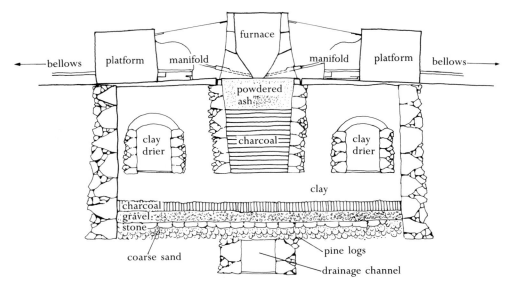

37. Cross-section of the NBTHK *tatara* at Shimane. The complex structure below the ground is for insulation, damp-proofing, and drainage. The clay driers are hollow; wood was burned in them at the time of construction.

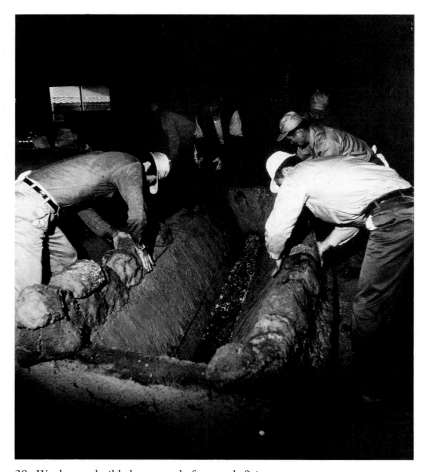

38. Workers rebuild the *tatara* before each firing.

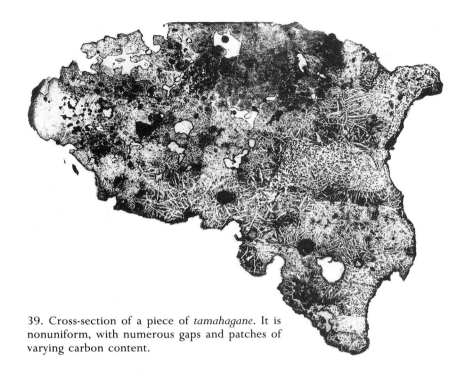

39. Cross-section of a piece of *tamahagane*. It is nonuniform, with numerous gaps and patches of varying carbon content.

coal is added. Thirty minutes later, iron sand and charcoal are dumped in again. In this way, *satetsu* and charcoal are added every half hour over the next seventy-two hours. If the firing were to continue any longer than this, the clay walls might corrode and collapse.

By the time the smelting cycle is complete, the *tatara* will have consumed 13 tons of charcoal and 8 tons of *satetsu*. The temperature at its highest will have reached 1200–1500°C, causing the impurities in the metal, which melt at a lower temperature than the iron, to liquefy and run out the slag holes. Meanwhile, the pure iron has been combining with carbon present in the charcoal.

What remains behind, at the bottom of the trough of the *tatara*, is 2 tons of iron and steel. This steel block is called the *kera*. The workers knock down the walls of the *tatara* and push the *kera* into position below a 30-foot tower. A large weight is then sent crushing down repeatedly from on high, breaking up the *kera* into about a dozen large pieces. Using sledgehammers, the workers pound these pieces of raw steel into smaller fist-sized chunks for inspection and sorting.

About half the *kera* is composed of steel ranging from 0.6 to 1.5 percent carbon, and it is this portion that is called *tamahagane*. About two-thirds of this is optimum quality steel of 1.0 to 1.2 percent carbon; the rest of the *tamahagane* is made usable by combining high- and low-carbon pieces during forging. The non-*tamahagane* half of the kera can be converted into usable stock by the addition or reduction of carbon in a separate forging operation called *oroshigane*. This is usually carried out by the smith at his shop (see below).

The carbon introduced into the raw iron ore by the burning of charcoal in the *tatara* is not evenly distributed throughout the *tamahagane*. While this nonuniformity would be unacceptable in factory steel, it is just what the Japanese sword requires. Differing degrees of hardness and softness (which is what carbon produces in the steel) mean that the finished metal blade absorbs shock better; as metallurgists say, it is tougher. Nothing could be more important on the field of battle. The varying carbon content also produces interesting visual effects on the metal surface, this being one of the focal points of sword appreciation among connoisseurs.

Through years of experience, swordsmiths like Yoshindo know at a glance the approximate carbon content of whatever piece of *tamahagane* they are holding. Good *tamahagane* will be dense and heavy, with a bright silvery color and fine crystalline structure. Poor *tamahagane* will look grayish black and coarse. Yellow, blue, and purple flecks that occur look like impurities but are merely the result of oxidation when the steel is first exposed to the air. When Yoshindo receives a shipment from Shimane, he can swiftly sort through it to determine its quality and likely properties during forging and hardening.

The Forge and the Bellows

We have already described how Yoshindo's forge is situated in his workshop, built into the earthen floor within convenient reach of the anvil and the power hammer. The channellike area between the firebrick walls of the forge is long enough to allow the entire length of the sword to be easily manipulated, and narrow enough (10 inches) to allow the coals to attain and hold very high temperatures.

Unlike Western forges, where the air blast comes from below, the air in the Japanese forge is introduced from one side. The bellows is a rectangular box about 3 feet long, 12 inches wide, and 18–24 inches high. It is usually to the left of the forge, behind a low concrete wall, so that the smith can work the piston of the bellows with his left hand as he manipulates the sword with his right.

Inside the bellows is an empty chamber divided in two by a vertical slab of wood that acts as a piston. Animal fur—raccoon fur to be precise—is traditionally used here as a gasket to allow the wooden piston to glide smoothly back and forth. When the smith pumps the piston, one-way flaps on the far and near side of the bellows alternately swing open to pull air into the chamber. As the air on one side of the piston is drawn in, the air on the other is compressed and forced out of the bellows through a narrow tuyère that leads directly to the forge. The action of the piston therefore produces a continuous blast of air. This is the significant design feature of the Japanese bellows and certainly one of the reasons for the high level of sword-making technology in Japan. The volume and speed of the air flow—and as a result the temperature of the coals—can be precisely controlled by the rate of pumping.

Pine charcoal from Kuji City in Iwate Prefecture is used in the smith's forge. One of the apprentice's main jobs is to chop each piece of charcoal with a cleaver and then filter these pieces through a chicken-wire mesh to separate them by size. Larger chunks are used for most of the work at the forge. Smaller chunks that burn with an intense and steady heat are used for hardening the edge (*yaki-ire*), when temperature control is all-important.

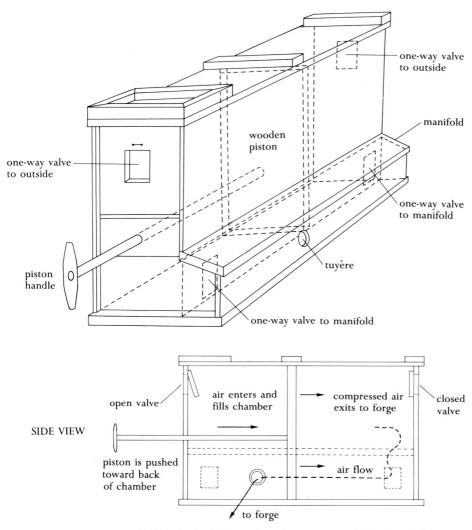

one-way valve
to outside

manifold

one-way valve
to outside

wooden
piston

one-way valve
to manifold

piston
handle

tuyère

one-way valve to manifold

SIDE VIEW

open valve

air enters and
fills chamber

compressed air
exits to forge

closed
valve

piston is pushed
toward back
of chamber

air flow

to forge

Air flow in the bellows when the piston is pushed and pulled.

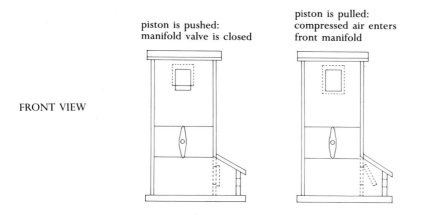

piston is pushed:
manifold valve is closed

piston is pulled:
compressed air enters
front manifold

FRONT VIEW

40. The swordsmith's bellows.

41. Larger pieces of charcoal (*right*) are used for forging, while smaller pieces are used for *yaki-ire*.

One of the greatest of contemporary smiths, Akihira Miyairi, was so particular that he would cut up each piece of *yaki-ire* charcoal by hand with a scissors instead of using, as Yoshindo does, a more vulgar strainer of chicken wire. Miyairi, it is said, spent so much time on cutting his charcoal and other details that he could make only two good swords a month—and since the postwar Japanese government chose his work as the model for the legal standard, no smith in Japan today is allowed to make more than that.

Oroshigane: Preparing the Steel

Yoshindo has to examine every shipment of *tamahagane* he receives from the NBTHK smelter in Shimane. Since he wants a final carbon content of about 0.7 percent in the "jacket steel"—called *kawagane*—that is used for the outer surface of the blade, and since forging produces a continuous loss of carbon, Yoshindo ideally wants to start with *tamahagane* that has a carbon content of anywhere from 1.0 to 1.5 percent. Sometimes the *tamahagane* Yoshindo receives has been presorted. In this case it is a simple matter for him to decide which pieces to use for the jacket of the blade and which to use for the softer steel—called *shingane*—at its core.

But many of the pieces Yoshindo gets from the *kera* are outside the optimum carbon-content range and cannot be used without further smelting. For example, steel approaching 1.7 percent carbon does not forge or weld well because when it is heated and hammered it tends to crumble. Some of the low-carbon steel (below 0.5 percent) can be used for *shingane*, but *shingane* is only needed in small amounts. This same steel is unsuitable for *kawagane* because it cannot be easily hardened; when mixed with steel of higher carbon content it produces unsightly blotches on the final surface of the blade.

Oroshigane is the name for two related processes that Yoshindo uses to adjust the carbon contents of these steels and make them suitable for sword manufacture. (It is also the name of the metals that result from these processes.) The method used with low-carbon steel is like that of the *tatara*. Yoshindo first spreads the bottom of his forge with finely powdered char-

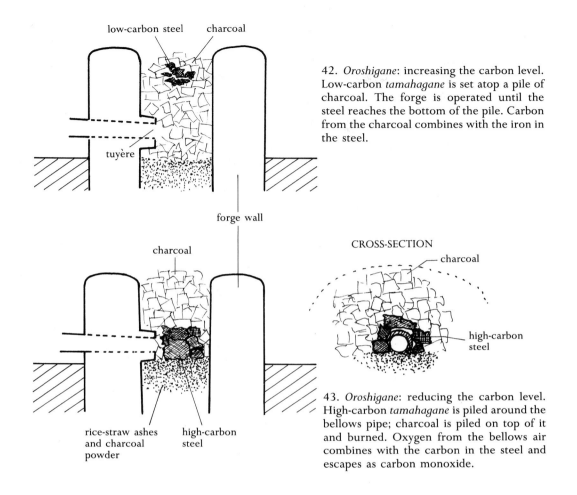

42. *Oroshigane*: increasing the carbon level. Low-carbon *tamahagane* is set atop a pile of charcoal. The forge is operated until the steel reaches the bottom of the pile. Carbon from the charcoal combines with the iron in the steel.

43. *Oroshigane*: reducing the carbon level. High-carbon *tamahagane* is piled around the bellows pipe; charcoal is piled on top of it and burned. Oxygen from the bellows air combines with the carbon in the steel and escapes as carbon monoxide.

coal. Then he adds larger charcoal pieces and sets them alight. Next he lays in a layer of low-carbon steel, followed by another layer of charcoal. He repeats this several times more, layering steel and charcoal over the forge. As the charcoal burns away, the hot steel settles down to the bottom of the forge, and as it does it combines with the carbon to produce high-carbon steel.

The method for high-carbon steel is somewhat different and exploits hot iron's tendency to release carbon in the presence of oxygen. Yoshindo spreads the bottom of the forge with rice-straw ashes mixed with charcoal powder (the rice-straw ashes act as a binder and prevent the powder from being dispersed by the bellows blast). Next he lays in a layer of high-carbon steel, mounding and hollowing it so that the pipe from the bellows will pump oxygen directly into the center of the pile. Above this he adds a load of charcoal. After lighting the coal Yoshindo pumps the bellows vigorously to maintain a steady stream of air into the glowing lumps of steel. The fresh oxygen combines with carbon in the steel and escapes as carbon dioxide. What remains in the forge is a metal whose reduced carbon content has made it more suitable for forging and welding.

Tsumiwakashi: Assembling the Steel Block for Forging

It is now time to refine the steel and start working it into a sword. Yoshindo takes chunks of *tamahagane* (or *oroshigane*), heats them in the forge, and hammers them into flat sheets a quarter of an inch thick. After cooling the sheets by quenching them in water, he uses a hammer to break them up into smaller wafers about an inch square. The color and carbon crystal size of these flat pieces of steel are readily visible in cross-section. Very bright and clear cross-sections are higher-carbon steels (more than 1 percent carbon). A darker, muddy color indicates a lower carbon content and possibly impurities. Yoshindo visually sorts through the *tamahagane* in this way, selecting the best pieces for the *kawagane* steel that will be used for the jacket of the blade.

Yoshindo next takes the wafers of *tamahagane* he has selected and arranges them in a stack atop a plate of steel he has welded to a long handle. This block of raw steel measures anywhere from 3 to 5 inches on a side and weighs 4 to 7 pounds. Yoshindo wraps the steel in clay and paper to hold it together and places it into the forge. He piles charcoal around the steel and heats it for thirty to forty minutes, removing it from the fire when it reaches a bright yellow or white color (1300°C). Placing the glowing block on the anvil, he gently hammers down on it to fuse all the wafers of *tamahagane* together. Yoshindo must work very deftly and quickly here, because the temperature of the steel begins to drop as soon as it leaves the fire; too much of a drop will make the separate pieces of steel impossible to weld.

The steel is now returned to the forge, heated and hammered again. The first hammering consolidated all of the small steel wafers and the plate that held them into a single block. Subsequent hammering gradually draws the block out into a bar that is about twice its original length. This requires several cycles of heating and hammering until the metal is too cool to work and needs to be returned to the forge.

44, 45. Flattened wafers of *tamahagane* are stacked on a steel plate to be welded into a steel block. The stack is then wrapped in paper to hold it together in the forge.

46, 47. A clay slurry and a coating of rice-straw ashes are applied
to the hot steel block to help prevent overheating, oxidation, and
the resultant loss of carbon.

Kitae: Forging

When the elongated bar is deemed ready, Yoshindo makes a deep cleft in it
with a chisel and folds the bar back upon itself, restoring it to its original
length. He now repeats the process of heating and hammering and heating
and hammering until the top and bottom halves have welded together and
the bar has again doubled in length (or width). Once more he folds it in half
and returns the steel to the forge.

Forging the steel at this stage is usually done with the power hammer. As
Yoshindo controls the speed of the hammer with his foot, he moves and
rotates the steel block so as to work it evenly on each surface. The power
hammer always strikes the anvil in the same place. Similarly, when using
three assistants with sledgehammers (as he does when working away from
his shop), Yoshindo makes sure that they strike the anvil in the center—it is
always the steel that moves. This is for obvious safety reasons, but it also
enables Yoshindo to position the hammer blow on the steel exactly where
he wants it. The hammer—and this is a basic rule of all forging—always
strikes with its head flush to the steel. While hammering, Yoshindo holds a
thick bundle of wet rice-straw in front of the steel to protect his face from
flying sparks and pieces of steel. Periodically he adds a few shovelfuls of charcoal to the area of the forge just in front of the bellows pipe.

48. The *tamahagane* has been welded together and drawn out into a bar. Yoshindo and his student make a chisel cut to begin folding the steel.

49. The cut steel bar can be folded by holding it against the edge of the anvil and hammering to bend it down at the notch.

50. The cut steel bar is folded completely over.

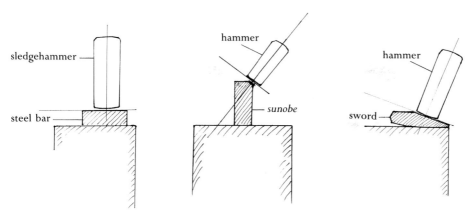

sledgehammer

steel bar

hammer

sunobe

hammer

sword

51. No matter what stage of forging, the hammer always strikes the steel perpendicular to its surface.

Yoshindo continues in this manner until the bar has been folded a total of six times. Each fold requires about thirty minutes and two or three "heats." Actual hammering can only be done for three or four minutes, until the yellow-white steel cools to bright red. While heating the steel, Yoshindo periodically removes it from the forge, quickly rolls it in rice-straw ashes, and covers it with a clay slurry before returning it to the fire. The clay and ashes help protect the steel by preventing oxygen from reaching its surface; this slows down the rate of carbon loss and oxidation. Were they not used, the combination of oxygen and high temperature would cause an extreme loss of carbon (reconverting the steel into iron), thus wasting a large amount of the material being worked. Even under normal conditions, the first stage of forging usually consumes about half of the original *tamahagane*.

These first six folds are called *shita-gitae*, or foundation forging, and produce a bar of steel with dimensions 10 × ¾ × 1½ inches weighing 2¼ to 3½ pounds. But at this stage the metal is still not ready; there is too much carbon, and it is not uniformly distributed. Before continuing forging, Yoshindo cuts the bar into three equal-sized pieces. Two of these pieces are enough for a small sword, while four (using an additional piece from another batch) will be needed for a full-sized blade.

Yoshindo piles the four pieces of foundation-forged steel on top of each other and, heating and hammering, welds them together. The resultant mass, weighing from 3¼ to 5½ pounds, is now hammered out and folded another six or seven times. This second set of folds is called *age-gitae*, or finish forging. Again, about half of the steel is lost. The result is a steel bar that weighs 2 to 3½ pounds with a carbon content of about 0.7 percent, the optimum as far as Yoshindo is concerned (smiths differ on this; Yoshindo's brother, Shoji, for example, likes his steel to be 0.6 percent carbon).

Most of the carbon in the *tamahagane*—as much as 0.3 percent—is lost during the first stage of forging, when the pieces of raw steel are flattened, stacked, and hammered together. Each successive fold causes a loss of 0.03 percent as large carbon crystals continue to be broken up. Suppose the starting *tamahagane* has a carbon content of 1.4 percent. By the time of the first fold, this has already been reduced to 1.1 percent. Thirteen more folds causes a loss of 0.03 percent $\times$ 13 = 0.39 percent. This leaves the final steel with a carbon content of about 0.7 percent. At the same time, the hammering and folding has also made the carbon distribution more uniform and forced out most of the large impurities and slag.

Yoshindo gauges all this by eye, examining how the steel looks as it is being worked. There is no prescribed number of folds, although in Yoshindo's case it is usually about thirteen times in all. The steel is ready when it folds continuously and smoothly with no splitting or cracking visible in the chisel cut. By carefully selecting his pieces of steel in the beginning and when assembling the bar for finish forging, and by observing the steel's behavior while he heats and hammers it, Yoshindo can produce exactly the type of steel he wants.

As important as the carbon content is the quality of the metal, the *jitetsu*, and its surface pattern, the *jihada*. The forged metal, having been folded thirteen times or more, becomes a kind of metallic pastry dough, consisting of

52. Cross-section of a cut bar of steel. The smoother sections were cut by the chisel. The rougher area in the middle is stretching from the folding. The gaps and pockets here indicate that this steel is still in a very early stage of forging.

53. Another cross-section, at a later stage in the forging. The central area is smooth with no large visible gaps or voids. The bar is almost ready to be formed into a blade.

54. Folds can alternate lengthwise and crosswise.

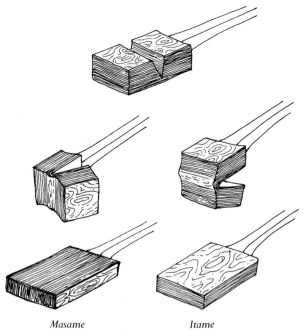

55. Two *jihada*. *Masame* grain is produced when the unhammered face of the forged block of steel is used to form the surface of the blade. *Itame*, which resembles a wood grain, is created by using the hammered face.

Masame   *Itame*

layer upon layer—some 16,000 or more—per inch of steel. The arrangement of these layers can be controlled, and on a well-polished blade they appear as distinct patterns. If at the beginning of finish forging the smith combines blocks of steel from different foundation-forged batches (which he often does), the different carbon steel strata will show up as contrasting lines along the unburnished sections of the final blade. Shinshinto smiths often used this technique to make very flashy-looking swords.

How the block of steel is hammered is more important in determining the overall pattern of the *jihada*. Folding in one direction only (lengthwise) and then hammering out the steel block so that its sides become the surface of the blade produces the straight-grain pattern called *masame*. The straight lines are in fact remnants of the original stack of *tamahagane* wafers.

The steel can be folded in one direction only, or it can be folded alternately lengthwise and crosswise. If the surface of the blade is formed from the top, hammered surface of a steel bar that has been folded only lengthwise, or if it is formed from any surface of a bar that has been folded both lengthwise and crosswise, the pattern that results is called *itame*. *Itame* looks like whorling wood grain, the result of sharp hammer strikes that have caused different layers of steel to be pounded through each other and intermix in complex patterns.

Subtle variations in these basic *jihada* can be produced by changing the strength of the hammer blows, the shape of the hammer head, and the temperature of the steel. Another kind of *jihada*—called *ayasugi*—appears as regular wavy lines. It is not produced by hammering but by selectively filing away sections at the edge of a *masame*-pattern steel block when the blank for the sword is being formed. Yoshindo feels this and other techniques that mechanically enhance the *jihada* are mere decorative artifice and never uses them on the blades he makes.

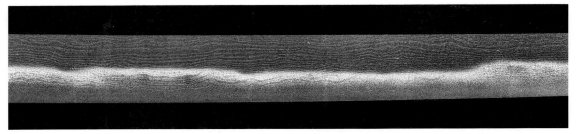

56. Simple *masame* grain.

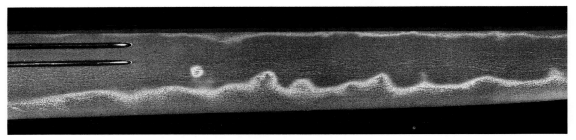

57. A more complex *masame*.

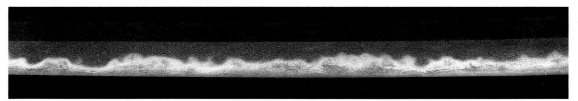

58. *Itame.* The pattern is skillfully enhanced by the inclusion of steel with higher carbon content. This shows up as dark lines or patches in the *ji*, an effect called *chikei*.

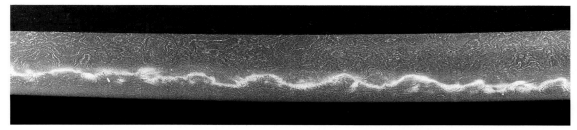

59. Another type of *itame.* Certain forging techniques can produce a very prominent *jihada*. Some collectors enjoy this look.

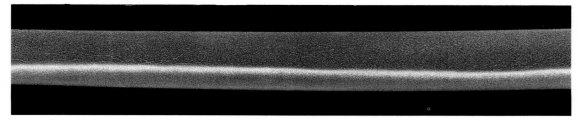

60. *Ko-itame,* or "small *itame*."

Shingane: Core Steel

The forging process described above is used to make *kawagane*, or jacket steel. This is the steel that will form the outer surface of the blade, including the sharp edge and the hamon. Daggers can be made entirely of *kawagane*. Medium- and full-size swords, however, are usually made of a composite of *kawagane* and a slightly softer, low-carbon steel called *shingane*, or "core steel." As its name implies, *shingane* is embedded or wrapped in the high-carbon jacket steel along the entire length of the sword. Being more ductile than *kawagane*, it helps protect the blade from cracking or breaking under stress.

To make *shingane*, Yoshindo begins with a 2-pound chunk of *tamahagane* that he knows has an average carbon content of about 0.5 percent. Instead of flattening it and making it into a stack of small wafers, however, he merely hammers the raw steel into a flat bar, which he then folds and refolds as many as ten times. *Shingane* has to be folded this much because it tends to be full of impurities. In the end, Yoshindo will have a long and narrow bar weighing about half a pound (that is, only a quarter of the original weight—the rest has been lost through forging) with a carbon content of 0.2–0.3 percent. Other steels with more or less carbon can be made by increasing or decreasing the number of folds with appropriate pieces of *tamahagane*. Some smiths, for example, will make a medium-hard steel to use on the sides or back of the blade.

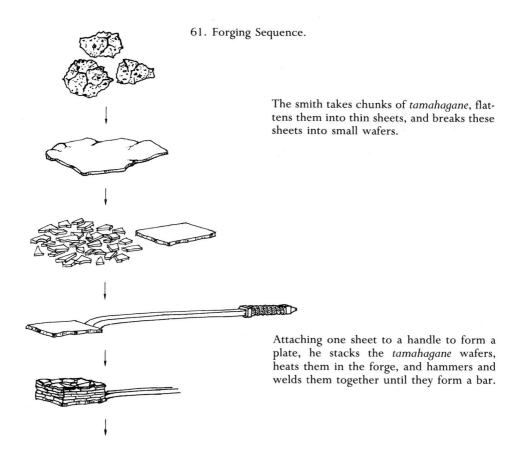

61. Forging Sequence.

The smith takes chunks of *tamahagane*, flattens them into thin sheets, and breaks these sheets into small wafers.

Attaching one sheet to a handle to form a plate, he stacks the *tamahagane* wafers, heats them in the forge, and hammers and welds them together until they form a bar.

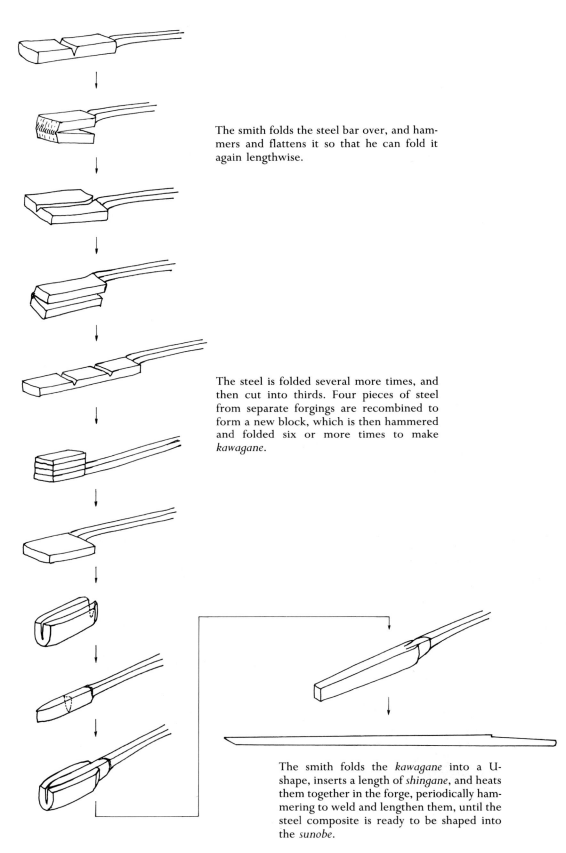

The smith folds the steel bar over, and hammers and flattens it so that he can fold it again lengthwise.

The steel is folded several more times, and then cut into thirds. Four pieces of steel from separate forgings are recombined to form a new block, which is then hammered and folded six or more times to make *kawagane*.

The smith folds the *kawagane* into a U-shape, inserts a length of *shingane*, and heats them together in the forge, periodically hammering to weld and lengthen them, until the steel composite is ready to be shaped into the *sunobe*.

Tsukurikomi: Forming the Steel Stock

The next step is to wrap the *shingane* in the *kawagane*. Yoshindo first hammers out a 2½-pound piece of *kawagane* into a flat plate about 15 inches long and bends it into a U shape along its entire length. He places the 1-pound *shingane* bar in the base of the U. The soft core steel doesn't quite extend to the part of the stock that will become the point, which is made only with the best and hardest steel.

Yoshindo now returns the two pieces to the forge, heats them until they are glowing a bright yellow (about 1300°C or higher), and begins hammering so that the *kawagane* completely encloses the *shingane*. The weld between the two must be complete and perfect. An error at this stage could produce gaps or voids inside the blade, or leave some *shingane* steel showing through on the surface. Either of these would be fatal in the construction of a Japanese sword.

This simple jacket-and-core-steel sandwich forging is called *kobuse-gitae* and is the most common form of sword construction. Another configuration is *hon-sanmai-gitae*. This consists of three separate pieces of high-carbon steel for the two sides and the edge. More complicated composites might use four or more different pieces of steel for the core, the edge, the sides, and the back of the blade—each of which must be attached in a separate welding operation. Sometimes these involve intricate layerings of high-, medium-, and low-carbon steels. The effects of these various combinations have never been fully analyzed. Presumably there are indeed differences in the amount of toughness, brittleness, hardness, and so on, but it is unlikely that the smiths who first forged these blades could have been fully aware of them. The great variety of forging methods is no doubt a reflection of the way schools developed in isolation from each other over the centuries. In some cases, complex welding schemes were the misguided attempts of smiths in the late Edo period to re-create the "lost secrets" of Koto masters.

62. Hard jacket steel (*kawagane*) is worked around a softer core steel (*shingane*).

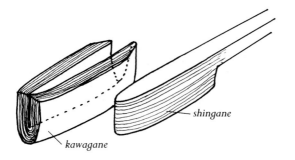

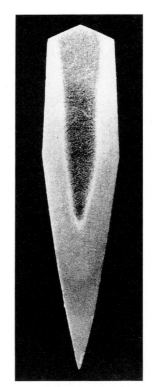

CROSS-SECTION

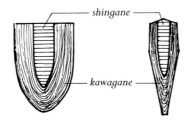

Composite Steel Bar   Forged Blade

63. *Kobuse-gitae* sword construction.

64. A *kobuse*-welded blade.

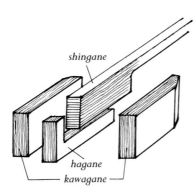

CROSS-SECTION

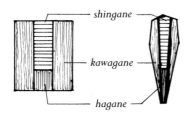

Composite Steel Bar   Forged Blade   Sharpened Blade

65. *Hon-sanmai-gitae* sword construction.
Hagane is "edge steel."

66. A *hon-sanmai*-welded blade.

Sunobe: Forming the Blank

Yoshindo now begins to form this composite steel bar into the blank, or *sunobe*, that will become the sword. He heats the bar in the forge and then hammers it into an oblong that is 90 percent as long as the intended final blade (to allow for expansion while forging). The width plus thickness of the blank at this point will be about 10 percent of the length of the final blade.

Yoshindo now partially hammers out the tang to distinguish it from the body of the blade: working alone with a hand-held hammer, he makes notches on the front (that is, the edge side) and back to define the position of the tang. He also rounds off and shapes the area that will become the point. Careful hammering throughout makes the *sunobe* uniformly thick from tang to tip and from front to back. It is still just a bar of steel, about 26–27 inches long, but it has the rough outline of a sword.

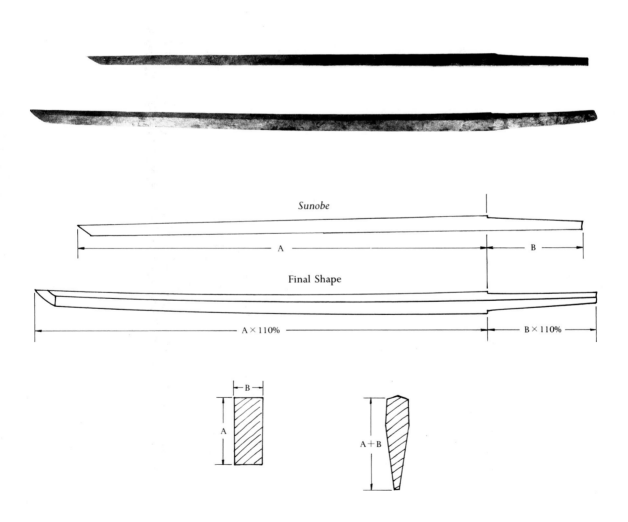

67, 68. The *sunobe* (top) is made shorter and thicker than the final blade to allow for expansion during forging.

Hizukuri: Shaping the Blade

Yoshindo draws the *sunobe* out perpendicular to its length, flattening it, that is, to begin forming the edge, the point, the ridgeline, and the back. Heating the blade until it is yellow (1100°C), he works at it steadily with his hand-held hammer until it is cherry red (700°C), and then returns it to the forge for reheating.

Only one section—about 6 inches—of the blank is heated at a time in the forge. This is a delicate stage, for if the *sunobe* gets too hot the hammer will spread the steel and destroy the metal composite; hammering when the steel is too cool could fracture the sword. Starting from one end, either the point or the tang, Yoshindo forms the edge and the ridgeline, working his way continuously along the blade to the other end.

This type of forging appears deceptively simple in the hands of an experienced smith. The blade appears to grow in a straight line as Yoshindo hammers it out, even though the steel on the edge, being thinner, is stretching far more than the steel along the back. Yoshindo works rapidly here, constantly rotating the steel to keep it from cooling where it touches the cold anvil. He hammers away at the top, the sides, the edge, and the back in rapid succession, varying the strength of each blow to produce just the right amount of expansion in the steel.

In the hands of a beginner very different things happen. The fledgling blade, rather than growing in a straight line, twists and turns and starts to look more like a snake than a sword. Every attempt to straighten it out seems to produce nothing but more curvature and wrinkles.

Yoshindo's uniform and even hammering produces a smooth surface and eliminates the need for extra filing and grinding later. The edge—which will ultimately be razor sharp—is at this stage left very thick, about a tenth of an inch. This is because final hardening and tempering are stressful and could crack the edge if it were too thin.

69. Yoshindo's son, Yoshikazu, uses a sledgehammer to help shape the blade from the *sunobe*. The tang end is very thick, and sometimes an assistant is required when working this part of the blade.

70. The smith has begun to form the edge and ridgeline on the *sunobe* by drawing the steel out perpendicular to its length.

71. The point area on the *sunobe*.

72. The point is shaped carefully with a hand-held hammer.

73. Having formed the blade, Yoshindo now works along its entire length with a hammer to smooth and shape the surface and straighten its lines.

Shiage: Rough Grinding and Filing

After forging, Yoshindo uses a two-handled drawknife along the sides of the blade to shave off any irregularities or unevenness in the surface of the metal. The drawknife, called a *sen*, works like a plane and has a piece of hardened, sharpened steel—usually from a section of a sword—as a blade. Yoshindo then uses files along the back and the edge of the sword, and follows this with a rough grinding using a coarse carborundum stone over the entire blade surface. The edge is not sharpened, however.

At this point the shape of the sword is very well defined, with all the lines and surfaces in place. Prominent now are the tang, the ridgeline, the *machi*, and the lines where the back meets the sides of the sword. The ground surface of the blade is kept very rough to enable the clay coating for *yaki-ire* to adhere well to it. As oil might also cause the clay to loosen, Yoshindo is careful from this point on not to touch any of the blade surfaces with his fingertips.

74. After forging, the shape is refined by filing and scraping.

75, 76. A two-handled, hardened steel drawknife called a *sen* is used to smooth the sides of the blade.

Tsuchioki: Making the Hamon

Copper is a metal that work hardens; as it is forged and worked by the smith, it becomes less and less malleable. Steel, however, hardens only by heating and rapid cooling. Hardened steel can be sharpened and will hold an edge, but it is unsuitable for the body of the blade because it is too brittle. For this reason, Japanese swordsmiths developed techniques for hardening only the cutting edge of the blade, leaving the body of the blade more flexible, able to absorb the shock of a blow or the stress caused by a sudden twisting.

The challenge for the smith here is twofold. First, the edge must be made hard enough, but neither too hard nor too soft. This depends on the firing temperature, the carbon content of the steel, and a number of other factors within the smith's technical control but never tested until the moment when the hot blade is quenched and cooled in water.

Second, as was explained in the introductory chapter, sword connoisseurship in Japan dictates that the blade display a recognizable pattern where the crystalline structure of the edge steel changes from hard martensite to soft pearlite. This pattern is the hamon; it is, to all intents and purposes, under the complete artistic control of the swordsmith. It is like a signature. The hamon is perhaps the most important aesthetic feature of a blade, and the first thing sword aficionados look for. B. W. Robinson's classic book, *The Arts of the Japanese Sword*, illustrates some fifty-three different hamon, each with its own name (from the descriptive "straight irregular" to the more suggestive "chrysanthemum and water") and the name of the smith or school identified with it. Tastes in hamon, like tastes in clothing, change over time. Today one of Yoshindo's favorite hamon is *choji*, or "clove blossom," a lobe-shaped pattern often associated with Bizen-style swords.

The hardened edge is produced by covering the blade in clay—thick along the back and upper portions, and very thin along the edge—heating it in the forge to between $700°$ and $900°C$, and then quenching it in a trough of water. Heating the blade over its critical temperature, it will be recalled, changes the phase of the steel to austenite. The final hardness of the steel thus depends on the speed at which it cools. If the steel cools rapidly from the quenching, as it does where the clay coating is thin, the austenite will change to martensite, and the metal will be harder than before. If the rate of cooling is slower, as it is where the thick clay coating serves as an insulator, the steel's structure will revert to its original ferrite and pearlite form, and the hardness of the steel will be relatively unchanged.

The exact pattern of the hardened edge is the result of three related variables:

1. The carbon content of the steel. Below 0.35 percent carbon, steel cannot practically be cooled rapidly enough to allow martensite— that is, a hamon—to form. Carbon content also affects the width and prominence of the line (the *habuchi*) that marks the border of the hamon. Steel of 0.6 percent carbon, which is what Yoshindo's brother, Shoji, likes to use, will produce a slightly wider border than the steel of 0.7 percent carbon that is Yoshindo's choice.

2. The clay coating on the blade. By controlling the placement and thickness of the clay, especially on or near the edge, the smith causes the differing crystalline structures of the steel to show up as recognizable patterns on the finished sword.
3. The temperatures to which various parts of the blade are heated. Deliberately or otherwise, all parts of the sword may not be at the same temperature before quenching. The edge, for example, is usually made uniformly hotter than the back along the entire length of the blade. These temperature values and variations help determine the appearance of the hamon and other visible properties of the metal such as *nie*, *nioi*, and *utsuri*.

Yoshindo begins by preparing the adhesive clay mixture that will be spread on the sword. This is made from clay, charcoal powder, and a pulverized sandstone (*omura*) in roughly equal proportions. Clay does the main job of insulating the blade. *Omura* stone prevents the clay from shrinking and cracking. Charcoal helps the smith adjust the rate of heating and cooling. The exact formula for the mixture may vary with the school and the individual smith.

Yoshindo adds water to the clay mixture and works it until it is suitably viscous. Using a spatula, he spreads clay onto the edge of the sword, scraping it off to leave a very thin layer where the hamon will be. Next, he spreads a much thicker—an eighth to a quarter of an inch—layer of clay along the upper portion and the back of the blade. This coating will prevent the blade from cooling rapidly and hardening. It will also determine the overall outline of the hamon. The outline will be stronger if the smith uses a thick ridge along the clay border to make a sharp demarcation between rapid- and slow-cooling sections of the metal.

Next, using the edge of the spatula over the clay layers he has already finished, Yoshindo applies a series of very thin strips of clay perpendicular or at angles to the edge of the sword. These strips serve as tiny insulators and create *ashi*, narrow channels of softer pearlite steel embedded in the hardened steel of the edge. Their toothlike pattern helps contain the extent of damage to a blade should the edge begin to chip: the chip will stop at the *ashi* line. *Ashi* can be an intrinsic part of the hamon design. Smiths working in the style of the Soshu school, however, add finely ground iron oxide to make the *ashi* in their hamon less visible on the final blade.

Each of these three steps of building up the clay is done in sequence: the edge, the sides and back, the *ashi*. A curious aspect of this procedure is that the blade is completely encased in clay, even though it might seem that if *yaki-ire* is successful because the edge cools quicker than the back, then the smith should not use any clay on the edge at all but leave it exposed directly to the cool water and the air. Actually, what happens is that the blade cools more rapidly *with* the thin clay coating. This is because the clay creates a larger surface area over the metal. It also prevents bubbles, which would become tiny insulators, from forming and remaining on the blade after quenching—these would leave visible spots of unhardened steel in the hamon.

Yoshindo now puts the blade aside for an hour or more to let the clay coating dry.

77. Yoshindo mixes the clay with water.

78, 79. The edge of the blade is coated first.

80. The upper portion of the blade is coated with a thick layer of clay.

81. Very thin strips of clay perpendicular to the edge create *ashi*.

82, 83. A freshly coated blade (*top*) and the same blade with the clay partially dry. The pattern formed by the dry edge is similar to what the hamon will look like after hardening; this pattern is *gunome*.

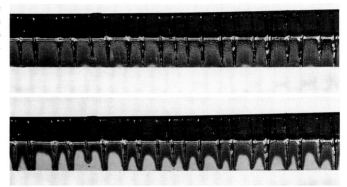

84, 85. Another example of a clay coating and the same blade, partially dry. The pattern here is *choji*, or "clove blossom," a typical Bizen-style hamon.

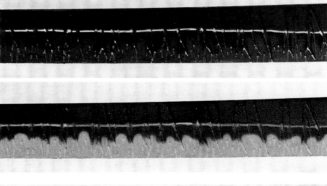

86, 87. A clay pattern for a straight hamon (*suguha*) and the same blade, partially dry.

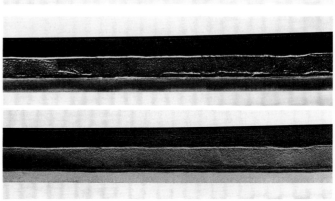

Yaki-ire: Hardening the Edge

Yaki-ire—the process of heating a sword until it is red hot, and then plunging it into a trough of water—is perhaps the most dramatic moment in the swordsmith's day. In the popular imagination, the glowing blade, the darkened smithy, the hissing billow of steam—all these make of *yaki-ire* an almost mystical enterprise, whereby the metal structure of the blade itself is transformed, and a sword is born.

The practical reality here, as is so often the case, is quite different. *Yaki-ire* is all in a day's work, and as often as not ends in a ruined blade that must be either reworked or discarded. It is performed at night with the lights out because the smith must be able to see the true color of the heated blade in order to judge its temperature. Tales of the quenching water having to come from such and such a mountain stream or having to be at such and such a temperature are perhaps fanciful, or part of the allure swordsmiths have always relied on to make their own techniques special or secret.

What cannot be denied, however, is that a successful *yaki-ire* demands considerable skill and complete intimacy with one's materials. The smith does not work from mass-produced factory steel. Every batch of metal he handles has unique properties, some of which the smith has intended, and others he must simply contend with. He judges the temperature of the blade entirely by eye, and then must not hesitate to seize the exact moment for quenching. Strict attentiveness followed by swift and uncompromised action is the hallmark of many Japanese crafts—the Zen calligrapher faced with a blank white paper comes most readily to mind—and does sometimes make one think the human artisan has been possessed by a spirit.

When talking about hardening Japanese swords, many Western writers use the term "tempering" and refer to the hamon as a "temper line." Technically, this usage is incorrect. It is more proper to say that the blade is heat-treated to harden the edge. Tempering is what is done after the hardening, to make the steel less brittle.

Yoshindo begins with small sugar-cube-sized pieces of charcoal to ensure a hot, even fire in the forge and to prevent physical damage to the clay coating that could alter the hamon. He wraps a rag around a bar of steel and wedges the tang of the blade into a U-shaped flange on the end of the bar. Holding the sword with the bar, he begins to draw the sword very slowly through the hot coals while steadily pumping the bellows with his left hand. The entire time, Yoshindo holds the sword with its edge up. As the blade heats up, it begins to glow. Yoshindo runs the sword through the fire ten to fifteen times, now and then letting the coals die down so that he can examine the color of the blade. When it is hot enough (over 700°C, between bright red and orange), Yoshindo turns the blade over and runs it through the forge again, this time with the edge down. After several more passes, the blade will be evenly and uniformly colored, and the edge (bright red to orange) will be heated to a higher temperature than the back (red to bright red). Yoshindo plunges the glowing blade into a trough of water.

Not all smiths do *yaki-ire* the same way. Smiths of the Soshu school of swordmaking, for example, mix white cast iron in with their steel to produce a spotty appearance in the final blade. They also wait until the blade is at a higher temperature before quenching.

THE SWORD: THE CRAFT 89

88. Yoshindo gradually heats the blade for *yaki-ire*, drawing it continuously through the fire.

89. Now the entire blade is glowing. After a few more passes in the forge, the blade will be ready for quenching.

90. *Yaki-ire*: the heated blade is plunged into a trough of water.

Yoshindo's method is particularly interesting in that it is designed to produce *utsuri*. *Utsuri*, meaning "reflection," is a whitish effect in the metal outside of the hamon on the side of the blade. Smiths in Bizen were renowned for it, but the technique was lost in Edo times. Because the *utsuri* pattern sometimes seems to follow that of the hardened edge, Edo-period connoisseurs called it a "second hamon." Technically this is incorrect, since *utsuri* shows no evidence of containing any martensite.

Utsuri points up the enormous skill of the smith for it only occurs under very specific conditions of temperature and metal composition. Yoshindo spent three years experimenting until he was able to re-create it, and now a few other modern smiths are making it as well. Basically, what the smith does is evenly heat the blade in three discrete longitudinal bands: The edge is heated to around 800°C. The back is heated to 700–720°C. The sides, where *utsuri* appears, are heated to 750–760°C—at this temperature the steel is in a transitional phase from pearlite to austenite; it is presumed that *utsuri* is related to the complex ferrite and pearlite microstructure that obtains in this area, although close scientific analysis has yet to be done. Failure to keep the blade within these narrow tolerances, or any unevenness in the temperature along the entire length and width of the metal, may produce an uneven or irregular hamon and *utsuri*, or no *utsuri* at all.

Temperature produces other effects as well, depending on the structure of the steel. We have seen how the smith can combine blocks of varying carbon contents before finish forging. Higher carbon layers will produce more martensite steel upon quenching, and these will be revealed by polishing as bright streaks in the pearlitic sword body called *kinsuji* and *inazuma*. If the carbon distribution throughout the blade is more heterogeneous, the quen-

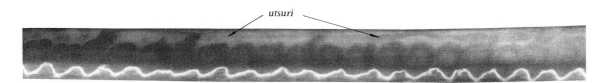

utsuri

91. A very clear example of *utsuri* on a Bizen blade.

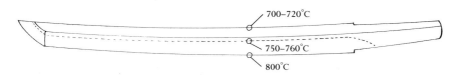

700–720°C
750–760°C
800°C

92. Temperature gradient for *yaki-ire* that will produce *utsuri* on a blade with a carbon content of 0.7 percent.

ching will produce bright grainy effects in the steel called *nie*, *aranie*, *nioi*, *konie*, and *sunagashi*—all patches of martensite but with different names according to their size or location. The longer the blade is heated the larger the size of the austenite grains that form and thus the larger the size of the martensite crystals that remain in the final blade. *Nie*, for example, appears as discrete and visible dots; it is produced when the grains of austenite grow sufficiently large. *Nioi*—described as being like snow, or white and misty—is produced at lower temperatures but represents a more durable blade: the higher temperatures used for *nie* can leave a sword brittle and prone to damage.

The *habuchi*, the whitish boundary line that defines the hamon, is in fact made up of *nie* or *nioi* (or of *konie*, in between the two in size). A hamon of some sort, therefore, can always be produced just by heating the clay-coated blade to a high enough temperature. But a hamon made without attention to detail might have blurred outlines or may not constitute any particular pattern. Sometimes one sees a blade where the hamon pattern is not uniform over the entire blade or is only recognizable in certain parts of the steel. This generally is the result of some sections of the blade being hotter than others at quenching. And while the source and temperature of the quenching water is not so important—Yoshindo uses regular tap water—at around 40°C the heat of the water begins to retard the cooling effect, thus weakening the hamon.

After *yaki-ire*, Yoshindo removes the sword from the water and runs it through the coals, reheating it to 160°C and quenching it again. This is called tempering (*yaki-modoshi*) and helps relieve stress in the hardened edge by partly decomposing the large, newly formed martensite steel

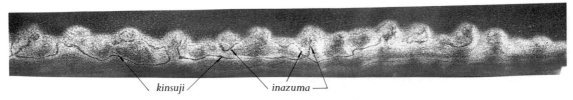

kinsuji   *inazuma*

93. *Kinsuji* and *inazuma* are both martensitic high-carbon areas that show up as bright streaks in the transitional zone (*habuchi*) between the hard edge and the pearlite body of the sword. *Kinsuji*, meaning "golden lines," is parallel to the length of the blade. *Inazuma*, meaning "lightning bolts," is usually zigzag and at an angle or perpendicular to the length.

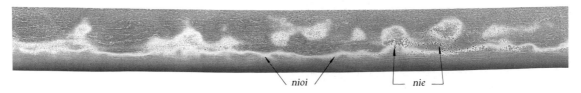

nioi   *nie*

94. Examples of *nie* and *nioi*, which are visible areas of martensite in the *habuchi* area. Compared with the misty, indistinct *nioi* areas, the areas of *nie* were heated longer at a higher temperature, thus creating large austenite crystals that resolved into discrete, visible particles upon quenching.

crystals. It also enhances the effect the polishing stones will have on the blade later. Tempering may be repeated several times. Yoshindo must be careful here, for if he reheats the blade to too high a temperature, part of the hamon could fade or disappear. This is what has happened to many antique swords retrieved from burning buildings: the metal is safe, but the hamon has been destroyed.

Yoshindo now takes the blade from the trough. Using a coarse, water-cooled grinding wheel, he removes all the clay and cleans the edge. He can make the hamon visible for inspection by applying a 2-percent solution of nitric acid. If the blade before quenching had been too hot, there might be cracks in the steel, or the hamon might be poorly defined. If the temperature of the blade had been too low, the hamon might not be present at all—meaning that the edge had failed to harden—or it might be misty and unclear (called a "sleepy hamon"). But if everything went as planned, the hamon will be bright and clear, with a distinct pattern in the exact shape Yoshindo had planned earlier when he applied the clay coating to the blade.

If Yoshindo is not satisfied with the hamon, he can remove it by heating the blade to a red color and then letting it cool slowly by itself in the air. This restores the entire blade to its original pearlitic structure. Yoshindo can then coat the blade with clay and repeat *yaki-ire*. A well-made sword will be able to withstand three to five such attempts. Yoshindo's success rate is comparatively high. About three-quarters of his blades survive *yaki-ire*. The figure for the average smith is probably about half or less.

95. After *yaki-ire*, Yoshindo uses a grinding wheel and removes the clay to examine the hamon.

GOOD

POOR

96. A good hamon has a well-defined shape and pattern over its entire length. Other details—such as *ashi* and *kinsuji*—make it more complex and visually interesting. A poor hamon indicates hardened steel but may be irregular, with no continuous or recognizable pattern.

Sorinaoshi: Adjusting the Curvature

During *yaki-ire*, the metal toward the back of the blade contracts for a longer period of time than the quickly cooled and newly hardened edge. This can increase the curve of the blade by almost half an inch. To compensate, the smith ideally forges the blade prior to *yaki-ire* with a curve that much less than the one he wants in the final blade. But usually some adjustment in curvature is necessary.

If there is too much curvature, Yoshindo can straighten the blade by hammering along the back ridge to expand the metal there. If the curvature is insufficient or uneven, he adjusts it by touching the back of the blade to a red-hot copper block and then quenching the sword in water. At each place he does so, a little local curvature is introduced into the blade.

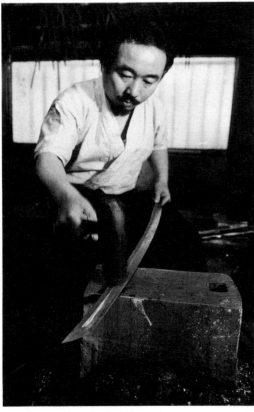

97. Hammering is sometimes required to straighten the blade.

98. Yoshindo holds the blade on a red-hot copper block and adjusts its curvature.

99. This blade has been heated four times in a narrow section along its back. The more often an area is heated, the larger the induced curvature.

Kajitogi: Rough Polishing

The size and main outlines of the sword were determined when the blank or *sunobe* was made. Now Yoshindo sets to work with his grinding wheel and a series of polishing stones to clean and contour all the lines: the ridgeline, the back, the sides. The edge is also ground down and sharpened.

Strictly speaking, the use of stones here is the work of the polisher, and is therefore covered in the next chapter. It is not at all unusual, however, for swordsmiths to give their own blades an initial rough polishing (up to the *kaisei* stage) before turning them over to an expert polisher for finishing. This assures the smith that the shape of the blade and the definition of its lines will be exactly as desired and will not be altered by the polisher. Also, cracks, poor welds, and other problems can often be detected in the early polishing stages. A smith would not want to pass on anything but a perfect blade to his fellow craftsmen.

100. Yoshindo gives the finished blade a rough polishing.

Hi: Decorative Grooves

Grooves (*hi*) are often cut into the roughly polished sword at this point. Traditionally, grooves are located above the ridgeline, where the metal is relatively soft. They are added for two reasons: as decoration and to lighten the blade. The width and shape of the grooves are up to the smith, but must harmonize with the overall design.

Cutting grooves is often the job of the apprentice. First he marks the location of each groove on the blade with a pen. Using a two-handled drawknife with a U-shaped blade of hardened steel, the apprentice works along the length of the groove, gradually cutting and deepening it. The rough groove is evened out with a round file, and then with a series of small carborundum stones and papers. Finally, the surface is burnished by rubbing it with a hard steel needle until it becomes bright and reflective. Cutting a good set of grooves in a long sword can take as much as two days.

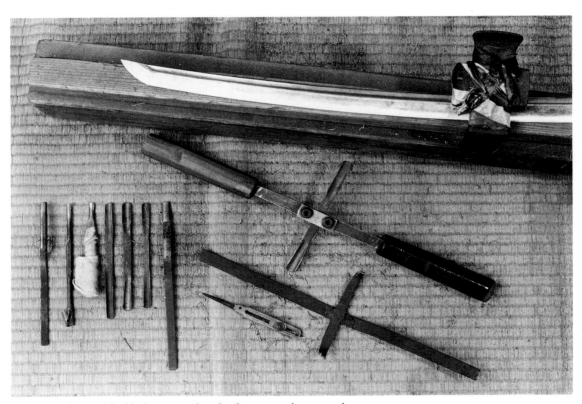

101. Interchangeable blades on a drawknife are used to cut decorative grooves in the sword.

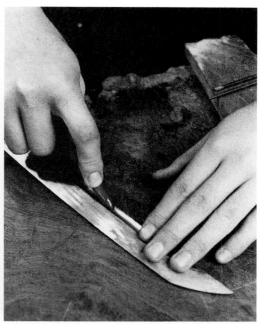

102. Yoshikazu cuts grooves into one of his father's new swords. The action of the drawknife is away from the body.

103. The inside of the groove is burnished with a steel needle.

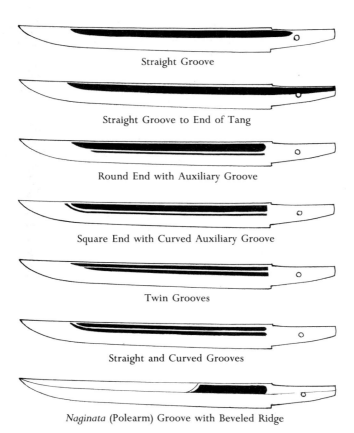

Straight Groove

Straight Groove to End of Tang

Round End with Auxiliary Groove

Square End with Curved Auxiliary Groove

Twin Grooves

Straight and Curved Grooves

Naginata (Polearm) Groove with Beveled Ridge

104. Common groove designs.

Horimono: Decorative Carvings

In addition to grooves, decorative carvings (*horimono*) can be added to the blade. *Horimono* designs are mostly traditional—cherry blossoms, bamboo, sword outlines, and dragons, as well as deities, Sanskrit characters, and other Buddhist motifs that point up the Japanese sword's original religious connection. The engraving is done with a small hammer and a series of very fine chisels. This is followed by burnishing. Making *horimono* is exacting, time-consuming work, and is often done by a specialist.

Yoshindo, like many swordsmiths, prefers to make his own *horimono*. He does not always stay with the traditional designs. His long sword entered in the 1984 NBTHK contest, for example, showed an engraving of a large tiger (Yoshindo jokingly called it his "Pink Panther"). This was an old design conventionally used in other Buddhist decorations, but never before on a sword. For that reason alone it displeased many people at the contest.

105. A decorative engraving (*horimono*) of a dragon is carved into the blade with a small chisel.

106. Yoshindo at work on a *horimono*. Note the number of chisels.

107. Yoshindo's *horimono* in the shape of a tiger.

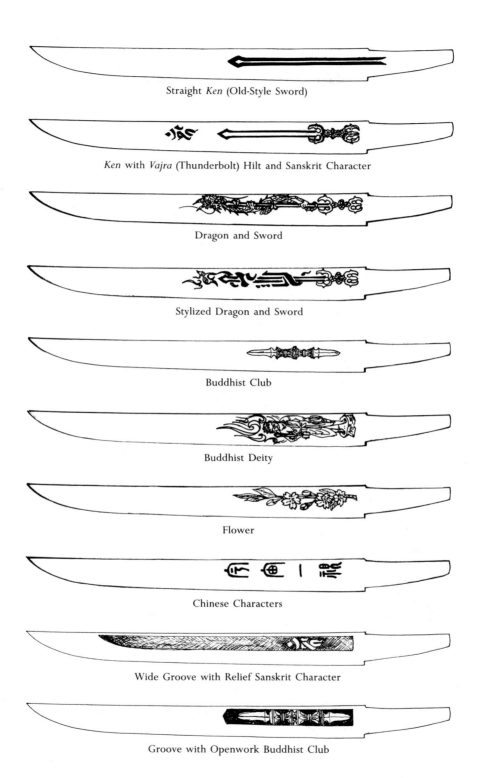

Straight *Ken* (Old-Style Sword)

Ken with *Vajra* (Thunderbolt) Hilt and Sanskrit Character

Dragon and Sword

Stylized Dragon and Sword

Buddhist Club

Buddhist Deity

Flower

Chinese Characters

Wide Groove with Relief Sanskrit Character

Groove with Openwork Buddhist Club

108. Common *horimono* designs.

Nakago: The Tang

The tang of a Japanese sword is finished with a decorative file pattern when it is made, but it is never polished or cleaned throughout the lifetime of the blade. Yoshindo's tangs are generally finished with a very coarse file whose marks leave a uniform slanting pattern in the steel. After filing, Yoshindo uses a drill press to open the *mekugi-ana*, the hole for the small rivet that passes through the tang and the hilt of the scabbard to secure the blade.

109. The tang is finished by filing.

Mei: The Signature

Now Yoshindo can send the sword out for its habaki, scabbard, and final polishing. He will sign the blade only when it is complete and passes his inspection in every detail. Using a small chisel and a hammer, he inscribes his name and any other information he or the owner might want into the tang. Examples of inscriptions are "Yoshindo," "Yoshindo *saku*" ("Made by Yoshindo"), or the place where Yoshindo lives, the date, and the name of the person for whom he made the blade.

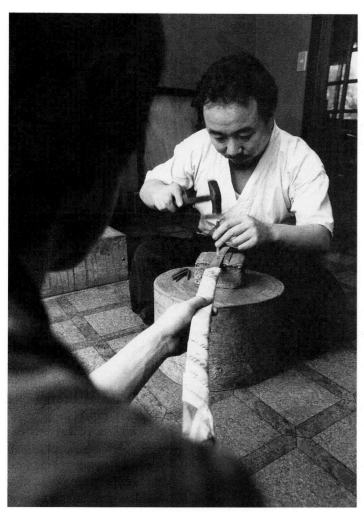

110. Yoshindo signs the blade after it returns from the polisher.

111. The chisel blade cuts the second character in Yoshindo's name.

OKISATO FUJISHIRO

Polishing

Centuries ago, when swords were still being used on the battlefields of Japan, it was the job of the polisher to put a sharp edge on the blade. This might take several days, depending on whether the sword was brand new or whether it had nicks and deformities that had to be repaired. Over the years, as the art sword has gained prominence, the job of the polisher has been transformed. The polisher continues to sharpen and clean the blade, but now, with an arsenal of small stones of ever-increasing fineness, he is able to make visible and attractive all the details of the smith's metalwork. It is the polisher who defines the lines of the blade, enlivens the hamon, brings out the grain of the steel (*jihada*), exposes its color and texture (*jitetsu*), and burnishes the top and back to a mirror finish.

Revealing the Blade

Polishing is an abrasive process. When the sword is made, all of the forging and the working and the hardening of the metal leave their mark somewhere in the final steel. If the surface of the steel could be made perfectly smooth, these marks would be easily visible. But the polishing stones, no matter how fine, always leave some kind of scratch on the steel surface. What the polisher does, then, is use a graduated series of stones, each one finer than the one before it, in such a way that the scratches left by the very last stone of the series will be so minute as to be actually smaller than the structural variations in the steel left by the smith.

The finish produced by a good polisher thus allows all the features of the blade to be seen clearly. This is essential to the fair appraisal of the sword's quality and provenance. A poor polish may produce a clean-looking blade, but its details may be cloudy, making careful examination impossible.

One of the reasons it is so difficult to trace the evolution of polishing in Japan is the nature of the medium: steel always rusts, regardless of how well it has been polished and maintained. A good polish will last no more than a hundred years. No one, therefore, knows what polishing in the Kamakura or Muromachi period was like because all extant blades have been polished

112. A polisher at work. From an Edo-period illustrated book.

in much more recent times. The few written descriptions we have from the past are either vague or confusing.

Originally, it was the swordsmiths themselves who did the rough polishing to make the edge and complete the final shape of the blade. They probably worked with the roughest grades of stone: *arato*, *binsui*, and *kaisei*. By the Kamakura period, polishers were already working separately from the smiths. References in old books to various features of the metal suggest that polishers were now using most of the stones used today.

By the Momoyama period, by virtue of their highly practiced eye for swords and their knowledge of past styles and craftsmen, polishers were also performing an important role as appraisers. Prominent among the appraisers was the Hon'ami family, who were established by the warlord Hideyoshi in the late sixteenth century and are still active in the Japanese sword world today. By declaring certain swords as valuable, the Hon'ami provided Hideyoshi with a ready source of rewards for his retainers and allies. The Hon'ami also served as official appraisers to the shogun in Edo. One of their most important tasks was the compilation, in the early eighteenth century, of a catalog of Japan's finest swords, the *Kyoho meibutsu cho*.

Polishing and appraisal are closely related. Japanese literature on polishing is full of phrases exhorting the artisan to "express the true character of the sword" and to "expose its heart." There is the idea here that a real sword lives beneath the metal surface, which the polisher slowly abrades away only so much and no more to reveal.

The polisher's understanding of the blade, however, takes place not merely on an aesthetic level but on the level of knowledge and tradition. A polisher must know what period a sword is from (or in the case of a new sword, what tradition it represents). He must know—or do his best to surmise—who its maker was, and all the characteristics of that maker and his school: the design of the hamon, the shape of the point, the quality of the metal, and so on.

At a certain point, too, the polisher must learn when a blade has had enough. An old sword may have been polished to the extent that its hamon barely remains; further polishing might destroy the hamon entirely. Similarly, removing a nick in the edge might result in grinding away the last part of a hamon; so sometimes the nick must remain.

A polisher must also develop a feel for the metal of different periods. How hard it is to remove scratches tells him how hard the steel is, an indication of its quality as well as its origin. The steel in swords made in the Bungo Takada region in the sixteenth century, for example, remains cloudy even when polished. To the inexperienced eye such a polish may look inferior; worse, in the hands of an inexperienced polisher such a blade can be irrevocably ruined by attempting to bring out its details more than the metal itself will allow.

The first job of the polisher, therefore, is always to ask, What kind of sword am I dealing with? Careful appraisal will point the way to the heart of the blade, and suggest how it can best be revealed.

The Polisher

Okisato Fujishiro (b. 1947) is the third generation in his family to become a sword polisher. He has recently joined his father as *mukansa*—that is, he is ranked above contest level. The Fujishiro family has also been well known as sword appraisers for several generations and publish a quarterly journal for connoisseurs called *Meito zukan*, or "Catalog of Fine Swords." Fujishiro's uncle Yoshio was one of Japan's great appraisers, a man who truly loved swords and knew them intimately. At the end of the war, when the Occupation authorities forbade swords to be made or possessed in Japan, Yoshio assumed that the Japanese sword and all he had lived for was over. One day he left Tokyo and just disappeared, and was never heard from again.

Fujishiro started looking seriously at swords from the age of eighteen. He had grown up watching polishers at work. His father, Matsuo, had never pressured him to follow in the tradition of the family, but when faced with a decision about whether to go to college, Fujishiro decided to stay home and become his father's student. This was a natural choice, for Matsuo was an accomplished craftsman and represented the main line of the Fujishiro family.

The Fujishiros represent one of the two main schools of polishing in Japan today, the other being that of the Hon'ami family, mentioned above. The two schools differ both in their training methods and in their finishing techniques. The Hon'ami are more strict about proper form and discipline: how the student is to sit, how he is to hold the blade, at how quick a pace he is to master the progression of stones. Hon'ami students, for example, spend two years on foundation polishing followed by two years on finish polishing before they are allowed to polish a single blade from beginning to end.

The Fujishiro school, in contrast, is far more relaxed about details and permits its students to progress rapidly from one stage to the next. This is how Fujishiro learned, and today he handles his own students the same way. Too much time on simple basics, he feels, might discourage the better students. Also, students who work on one sword from start to finish quickly learn where their basic mistakes occur. Errors early on in the polishing process sometimes don't show up until the later stages, and students should have the chance to see this.

When Fujishiro started out, the first thing he began to do was make *oshigata* and do appraisals. An *oshigata* is a tracing of a sword outline with the hamon carefully drawn in by hand. Because proper *oshigata* may take as many as ten hours to complete, not many polishers make them. But they are enormously beneficial to Fujishiro's work. They train him to look carefully at the blade and give him a much better sense of its detail. According to Yoshindo, once Fujishiro makes an *oshigata* of a hamon he never forgets it, much as if he had the fingerprint of the smith himself on file.

In 1972, Fujishiro got married and, following custom, brought his wife into his father's home. Four years later, after Fujishiro's second child was born, his father moved out of the house to set up a new shop in a different location—the reverse of standard practice in Japan. Matsuo knew that his own customers would follow him to his new shop, while his son would benefit from the existing location of the old one, particularly with its sidewalk location generating a fair amount of walk-in business.

Fujishiro thus became independent rather early by Japanese standards. Normally a student will stay with his teacher for ten or more years. But Fujishiro feels that having to support himself so soon made him worry more about improving his work. The shop's location—only a hundred yards from Ichigaya Station in central Tokyo—was also a boon, because casual customers often brought in a cheaper kind of sword that Fujishiro could use to refine his technique without having to worry so much about making a big mistake on a valuable blade.

The land Fujishiro's shop stood on was recently bought by a developer to make room for an apartment building. Fujishiro was given an apartment in the building and now maintains a new shop on the ground floor, still close to the street traffic. Three students share his household. Like Yoshindo's students, they live and eat with the family and receive room and board and some spending money. Students must be prepared to stay as long as ten years, but it is Fujishiro who decides when they are ready to graduate and set up their own shops.

Polishing requires a great deal of patience and talent. Talent, at least, tends to manifest itself quickly, so students do not end up wasting years in pursuit of a craft for which they have no aptitude. Fujishiro usually starts his students off with *uchigumori* stones, very fine stones with which it would be difficult to ruin a blade. At the next stage of their training, Fujishiro gives them a *chu-nagura* stone, still relatively fine but just coarse enough to remove rust from old blades. The most difficult stones, Fujishiro feels, are the very first three, the coarsest ones: *arato*, *binsui*, and *kaisei*. Used improperly, they will destroy the surface and lines of the blade.

Fujishiro works every day from nine to six for about ten days to do a good job on a long sword. But this is not all he does. In the evenings he might polish some more, draw *oshigata*, work on appraisals, or write for his sword journal. He only takes off Sundays, when he might indulge in his hobby of photographing astronomical phenomena—and taking close-ups of sword blades.

THE CRAFT

The working position of the Japanese polisher will be uncomfortable for anyone not used to it. The polisher sits on a low stool, hunched forward as he pushes the blade across the polishing stone. His right knee is wedged up into his right shoulder, while the weight of his right heel presses down on a curved piece of wood (the *fumaegi*) whose hook-shaped other end serves to clamp the polishing stone to the work block. His left foot is curled beneath his body as a brace to prevent the *fumaegi* from moving as he works.

Seemingly awkward, this position has the advantage of placing the polisher directly over the stone where he can precisely control the direction, pressure, and angle of the sword against its abrasive surface. Since water must be constantly applied as a lubricant, a bucket is kept close at hand (the entire polishing area is in fact a separate low-walled wooden enclosure, with a slightly sloping floor for drainage). The clamp that holds the stone in place can be removed simply by letting up on the right foot, enabling the stones to be changed quickly and as often as necessary.

113. The normal position for foundation polishing.

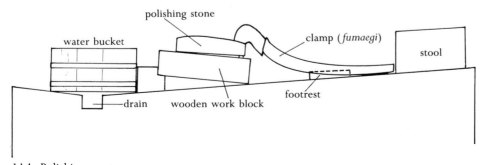

114. Polishing area.

Fujishiro has hundreds of polishing stones, of all different grades. Natural stones are sedimentary rocks like sandstone or limestone. Contaminants—in the form of pieces of granite or other bits of mineral silt washed into ancient seabeds—are a great danger here, for any hard grains in the stone will immediately scratch the sword and ruin the polisher's work. Good-quality stones are rare; the mountain quarries that supply them in Japan have all been known and in operation for a century or more.

Today, in the early stages of polishing, coarse artificial stones made from silicon carbide (carborundum) or aluminum oxide are often used in place of natural stones because of their availability and more uniform grain size. Polishing in the later stages, however, when extremely fine abrasive action is required, still depends on quarried stones. These are expensive. Their cost is a function of size, grade, rarity, and quality. Thick natural stones, which are more expensive per gram, can easily cost a thousand dollars or more.

Sword polishing has two basic levels. The first is called *shitaji* polishing, or foundation polishing. Here the blade is moved over the larger and coarser of the polishing stones (*arato* through *uchigumori*). The second level is called *shiage* polishing, or finish polishing. Here the stones used are very thin shavings backed with paper and lacquer. They are moved over the blade, which is held stationary in the hand. Polishing concludes with defining the point, whitening the hamon (using a *hadori* stone), and burnishing the back and upper sides.

Shitajitogi: Foundation Polishing

Yoshindo—like many other smiths—does most of the foundation polishing for his own swords, handing them over to Fujishiro or another polisher only after he is satisfied that all the lines and surfaces are correct in every dimension. The stones used at this stage are relatively coarse and rough. The blade must be moved across them with great precision and control to prevent deep scratches that no reasonable amount of polishing will remove. Because the surface of the blade is curved, the polisher must always be aware of how

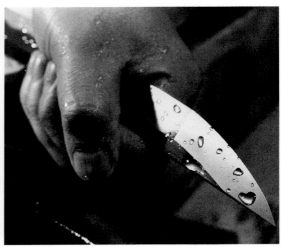

115, 116. During foundation polishing, the blade is moved over the stone.

much of the blade is in contact with the stone at any one time. The area around the ridgeline demands special concentration. Letting the stone slip over the ridgeline will dull it and possibly ruin the sword's appearance by changing its geometry.

While working on the sword the polisher tries to keep his back straight and his body positioned directly over the blade as he moves his arms back and forth. He holds the sword with a rag in his right hand and bare-handed in his left, the palm resting on the upper surface of the blade and the fingertips on the bottom. The fingers wrap around the blade but never exert pressure directly on the sharpened edge. For safety, the edge always faces away from the body. Thus, the polisher begins with the tang on his right; to work the opposite surface he flips the blade over so that the tang is on his left.

The blade is worked along one 4- to 5-inch section at a time. Any wider an area than this would be too hard to control. The polisher works systematically, from the tang to the point and then down the other side, concentrating on only one surface at a time: (1) the back (the *mune*), (2) the ridgeline to the back (the *shinogiji*), and (3) the edge to the ridgeline (the *ji*). Since each surface is polished somewhat differently, working only one section at a time makes it easier for the polisher to move with a consistent motion and pressure. From the edge to the ridgeline the work is more laborious, for the goal is to bring out the hamon and the texture of the steel. In the other two areas, because burnishing will hide the details of the steel, it is enough that the lines be true and the surfaces be smooth and clean.

The stages outlined here are the major ones in the polishing process. In practice, polishers use many kinds of intermediate stones while they work, or use similar kinds of stones that vary only slightly in coarseness. Each blade makes its own demands.

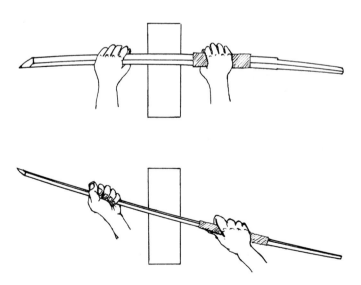

117. Hand positions used during foundation polishing for (*top*) the surface and ridge areas and (*bottom*) the back of the blade.

Arato

Fujishiro uses the *arato* stone only for new swords or older swords that are badly damaged or very rusty. It is made of a coarse natural sandstone (or a very coarse grade—180 grit—of carborundum stone). The *arato* removes all the file marks from the smith's work, sharpens the edge, and smooths and straightens all the lines of the ridge, the back, and the edge.

Fujishiro always moves the blade perpendicular to its length across the *arato* stone. As he works he constantly dabbles water onto the stone for lubrication. The coarseness of the polishing in this first stage creates scratches on the blade surface, and does not reveal any details of the steel.

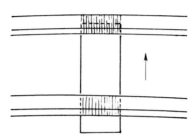

118. *Arato*. The marks of the stone are nearly perpendicular. Here and in following figures, the arrow shows how the blade moves in relation to the stone.

Binsui

Binsui is another coarse sandstone (equivalent to 280–320 grit) that Fujishiro uses to remove the marks left by the *arato*. His main concern at this early stage is still the overall geometry of the blade, the trueness and definition of its lines.

This time, rather than move the blade perpendicular to its length as he did with the *arato*, Fujishiro moves the blade against the stone at a small angle off the perpendicular. This is done to distinguish the new marks from the coarser marks left by the previous stone. Action diagonal to or along the length of the blade also leaves less deep scratches than action across the blade. In two respects, then, the coarseness of the stone and the angle of the polishing, Fujishiro has begun to refine the surface of the metal. (The point area is always polished perpendicular to the length of the blade, no matter which stone is used. Its surface curving in two directions and coming to a sharp tip makes working it with big stones very complex and difficult.)

When all the perpendicular marks from the *arato* are gone, and only the *binsui* marks are visible, Fujishiro will move on to the *kaisei* stone.

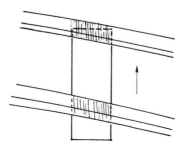

119. *Binsui*. The marks are finer and slightly diagonal.

Kaisei

Fujishiro moves the sword diagonally against the *kaisei* stone (400–600 grit), and at a 25° angle, again to allow him to distinguish new marks from *binsui* ones. He is starting to make the surface smoother and finer. The metal is getting darker and more reflective. The outline of the hamon becomes visible.

But Fujishiro is still primarily concerned with the shape of the blade. By the end of the *kaisei* stage, all the lines and surfaces will have a geometry that will not be changed by the succeeding finer stones.

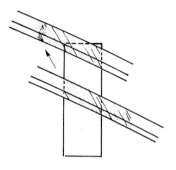

120. *Kaisei.* The sword is moved at a 25° angle against the stone and at a 20° angle to its length.

Nagura

There are two *nagura* stones, the coarser *chu-nagura* (800 grit) and the finer *koma-nagura* (1,200–1,500 grit). Depending on the polisher, these stones can be either natural or artificial. In Fujishiro's case, he will use either a natural or an artificial *chu-nagura* stone, but he will use only a natural stone for *koma-nagura*.

Both stones are used in the same manner, with the blade moving lengthwise along the stone in a slight rocking motion, power being transmitted along the forward stroke. Lengthwise strokes cut less deeply than diagonal ones, so rocking is used with the *nagura* stones to put the blade under considerable abrasive pressure. After each stroke, Fujishiro slightly rotates the blade to work gradually from the edge to the ridgeline. When one section of blade is finished he moves on to the next, gradually working his way up the blade from the tang end to the point.

When the diagonal *kaisei* marks are gone and the visible work marks are all lengthwise along the blade, Fujishiro moves on to the *koma-nagura* stone. Since this stone is only slightly finer than the *chu-nagura* there will only be a slight change in the metal. But at this stage the hamon has usually become clearly visible.

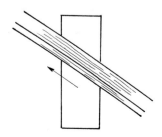

121. *Chu-nagura.* From this stage on, the stones are used along the length of the blade.

Uchigumori

From this stage on only natural stones are used. The polisher must always be on the lookout for small defects beneath the surface of the stone that can scratch a blade. There are two types of *uchigumori* stone: *uchigumori-ha-to* and *uchigumori-ji-to*. Both are much finer than the *nagura* stones, the equivalent of 3,000 grit or more, but the specific fineness used will depend on the particular sword. Different swords polish in different ways as a result of their shape, their carbon content, and the tightness of their welds. A polisher will keep several different grades of *uchigumori* on hand so that he can try one and then switch to another if that seems to give better results. Experience is his only guide, coupled with his sense of how he wants the final blade to appear.

Fujishiro moves the blade lengthwise along the *uchigumori* stone, holding it flat and not rocking it as with the *nagura* stones. *Uchigumori* stones are relatively hard, so all of the action of the blade along the stone is focused on the return stroke. This produces a straighter stroke and also, because the pressure is less than it would be on a forward stroke, makes it less likely that the blade will scratch.

Uchigumori-ha-to is used first on all of the blade's surfaces until the heavier, wider marks of the *nagura* are completely gone and the hamon is clear.

Uchigumori-ji-to is next. It is used only on the edge and the sides (the *ji*) to expose traces of the *jihada* along the blade surface just above the hamon. The back and the area above the ridgeline are omitted from this point on, as they will be burnished and don't need such a fine polish.

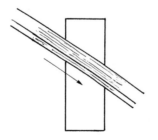

122. *Uchigumori-ha-to*. At this stage, the hamon should be free of all scratches and stone marks.

FOUNDATION POLISHING SEQUENCE
EFFECTS ON BLADE SURFACE AND MAGNIFIED VIEWS

123, 124. *Arato.*

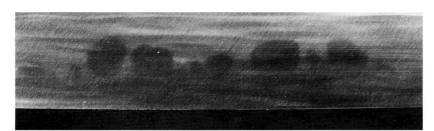

125, 126. *Binsui.*

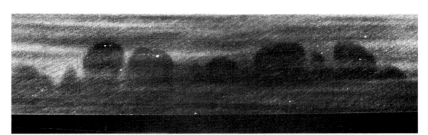

127, 128. *Kaisei.*

129, 130. *Chu-nagura.*

131, 132. *Koma-nagura.*

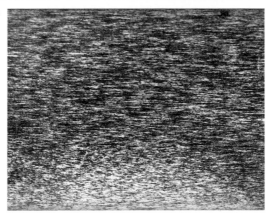

133, 134. *Uchigumori-ha-to.*

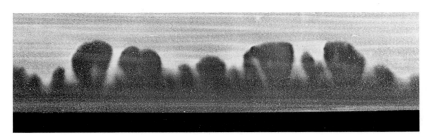

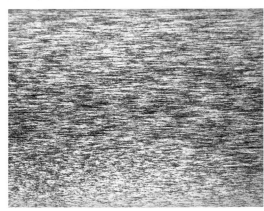

135, 136. *Uchigumori-ji-to.*

Shiagetogi: Finish Polishing

In the final polishing stage the polisher uses ever finer abrasive materials. The stones here are more like translucent paper-thin wafers. The polisher holds them in position with his thumb as he moves them over the surface of the stationary blade. The fine details of the hamon and the steel become more visible now, including *utsuri* and effects of the hardening like *nie* and *nioi*. The sum total of these details define the blade's individuality and demonstrate the control of the smith over his materials. A poor polishing job will cloud rather than reveal these important features of the metal.

Hazuya

Hazuya stones are actually very thin wafers of *uchigumori* made from pieces of *uchigumori* stone a third to a quarter of an inch thick that Fujishiro has removed with a saw. Fujishiro grinds these pieces of *uchigumori* on a rough sandstone until they are a uniform thickness of about a sixteenth of an inch. He then polishes them against a finer stone to give them a smooth surface. Mentally he sorts them out according to relative hardness, based on how they work against the stones.

137. Stones used for finish polishing: (*a*) slice of *uchigumori* stone with paper and lacquer backing, (*b*) the same paper-backed stone, ground down to 0.005 inches in thickness, (*c*) *hazuya* stone cut into a square, (*d*) *hadori* stone, like *hazuya* but smaller and oval so that it can easily trace the hamon, (*e*) *jizuya* stone, with surface cracked in a checkerboard pattern.

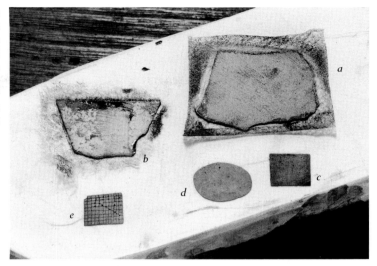

138. With finish-polishing stones, the backs of the fore- and middle fingers rest on the back surface of the blade.

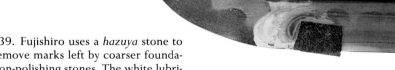

139. Fujishiro uses a *hazuya* stone to remove marks left by coarser foundation-polishing stones. The white lubricant is *tojiru*.

Fujishiro now picks up a *hazuya* stone and coats one face of it with a lacquer (*urushi*). He applies a piece of porous Japanese paper (*yoshino-gami*) to the tacky lacquered surface and adds another coat of lacquer. This paper backing has been previously impregnated with persimmon tannin, which helps it form a very hard surface that will support the stone and prevent it from crumbling during polishing. When the lacquer is dry Fujishiro grinds the stone down further and cuts it with a scissors or a knife into several small squares, about a half an inch to an inch on a side.

Before beginning with the square *hazuya*, Fujishiro rounds off its edges to make sure they are smooth and thin (0.005 inch). Then he makes a thin lubricating paste (called *tojiru*) by rubbing two wet *uchigumori* stones together. Finally he puts a small amount of this paste and water directly onto the area of the blade he is about to polish. Sodium carbonate is added to the water to keep it alkaline so that the wet steel surface will not rust.

Fujishiro rests the blade on a stand as he holds it steady with his left hand. Curling the forefinger and middle finger of his right hand into a fist, he places them against the back of the blade to serve as a guide for the *hazuya*, which is held between his right thumb and the blade.

Moving the stone lengthwise along the blade in tiny back-and-forth motions, Fujishiro polishes one section of the sword at a time, beginning at the ridgeline and moving down to the edge, working from the tang end up toward the point. The point is not polished at this stage, however.

The *hazuya* removes all of the marks left by the *uchigumori*. The blade takes on a whitish, cloudy appearance. There should be no marks or blemishes remaining in the hamon or the steel now. The surface of the blade must be smooth and uniform. If the earlier polishing steps were done well, very little time will be needed for the *hazuya*.

Jizuya

The yellow-brown or orange *jizuya* stone is used in the same way as the *hazuya*. It is made by chiseling off flakes from a *narutaki* stone—similar to *uchigumori* but a bit harder and finer—and then, as with the *hazuya*, grinding the flakes down and backing them with paper and lacquer.

There is considerable variation in the hardness of the stones at this stage, and Fujishiro, depending on the blade, may need three or more. Before using the *jizuya* he folds and cracks it several times vertically and horizontally to create a checkerboard pattern of lines on its surface. The paper backing remains intact. These cracks improve the stone's coverage and following of the blade surface.

As Fujishiro uses the *jizuya*, the blade becomes darker and clearer and the *jihada* begins to stand out. Which grade of *jizuya* Fujishiro chooses at this stage will greatly affect the final color, texture, and detail of the steel.

Nugui

The final step in polishing the surface of the blade is an application of *nugui*. This is a fine suspension of iron oxide particles in vegetable oil. When steel is heated to a bright red or yellow color, a film of black iron oxide forms on its surface. The iron oxide flakes or peels off easily when struck with a hammer. These flakes can then be collected and ground into a fine powder, called *kanahada*. Some polishers make their own *kanahada*, but it is also available commercially.

Fujishiro mixes a pinch of *kanahada* with clove oil and strains the resulting *nugui* through several layers of paper (*yoshino-gami*) to filter out any large oxide particles that might scratch the blade. He then applies a small amount of the filtered *nugui* directly to the surface of the sword and rubs it with cotton. He goes over the entire blade this way, section by section, one to three times depending on the effect he wants. *Nugui* is not used on the point area at all.

140. *Nugui*, an iron-oxide suspension, is used as a very fine abrasive. It is filtered through a piece of paper to remove larger oxide particles that could scratch the blade.

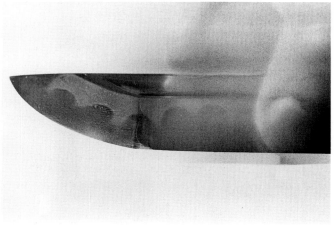

141. *Nugui* is rubbed over the surface of the blade with a piece of cotton. The surface darkens as the blade's surface details become more visible.

While there is a slight polishing action, the main effect of the *nugui* is cosmetic: it darkens the steel and thus highlights the metal grain and other surface details. Too much *nugui* will turn the metal black. In the past, disreputable polishers may have darkened the steel considerably to make a blade look older or added mercury or other chemicals to the suspension to etch the visible grain and make it showy.

Hadori

The different steels in a blade create a natural contrast between the *ha*, the hardened edge, and the *ji*, the sides. Depending on the individual sword and the techniques of the polisher, this contrast is more or less visible. Because sword connoisseurs today favor a very strong hamon, polishers often use one more step, called *hadori*, to produce a white, highly contrasting edge.

Fujishiro takes a *hazuya*—like the one he used previously—and cuts it into an oval shape. This eliminates any sharp corners that might scratch the blade and also makes the stone easier to direct along the contours of the hamon. Beginning at the tang end of the hardened edge, he applies some *to-jiru* and, while making small back-and-forth polishing strokes, uses the stone to follow the path of the hamon along the edge of the *habuchi* all the way up to the point.

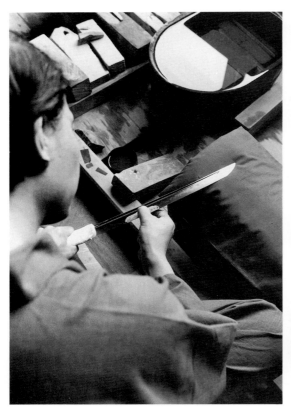

142, 143. The *hadori* stone is held in the same manner as the *hazuya* and *jizuya* stones.

The *hadori* (*hazuya*) stone is coarser than the previous *jizuya* stone and *nugui* finish. Its scratches are therefore larger and appear white against the rest of the blade. The hard hamon whitens quite slowly; it might take the polisher as much as two days to complete *hadori* for a single long sword. How closely the trail of the stone follows the actual hamon will depend on the skill of the polisher and the effect he wants to obtain. If the hamon consists of a small *choji* or *gunome* pattern, that is, one with tiny clefts and undulations, Fujishiro may use the *hadori* stone to group the smaller parts of the hamon into a single white wave. But if the hamon is straight (*suguha*) or has large lobes, he may follow it exactly.

Fashion (and, it is said, NBTHK judges) generally dictates that the hamon be white. Unfortunately, the whitening effect of *hadori* masks some of the finer details that are an inherent part of the steel and of the *habuchi*. On some blades, such as with Soshu-type work where the boundary between the edge and the rest of the blade is very indistinct anyway, *hadori* does improve the appearance of a blade. In Yoshindo's case, where that boundary is very clear and well defined, *hadori* is less necessary.

Hadori is used to enhance the appearance of the hamon. Here the pattern desired on the blade was a perfectly straight line, even though the actual hamon is irregular.

The polisher traces the outline of the hamon, but omits the parts of it that would make the *hadori* pattern too large or irregular.

the line here would be too broad and flashy

the line here would be too abrupt

One blade, two possible *hadori* patterns. The upper pattern has large straight areas with occasional dips. The lower one follows the real hamon as closely as possible.

144. *Hadori* patterns.

Collectors more interested in craftsmanship and metalwork generally prefer that the *hadori* step be omitted. In its place, polishers use a finish that emphasizes all the details of the hamon. This is called *sashikomi* and requires a slightly different *nugui* after the *jizuya* stone. The *nugui* for *sashikomi* is a suspension of finely ground minerals—*tsushima* (a limestone), ground iron ore, or *kujaku* (lodestone)—in clove oil and will selectively darken the *ji* but not the hamon, thus allowing the hamon to stand out sharply with all the details of its structure clearly visible. Which suspension is used depends on the individual sword.

FINISH POLISHING SEQUENCE
EFFECTS ON BLADE SURFACE AND MAGNIFIED VIEWS

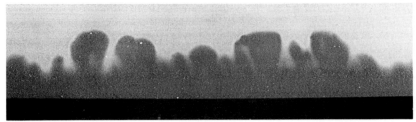

145, 146. *Hazuya.*

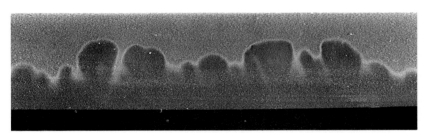

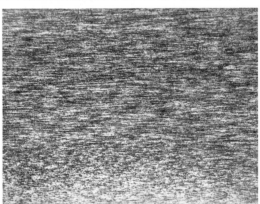

147, 148. *Jizuya.*

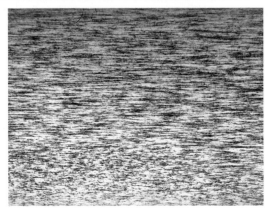

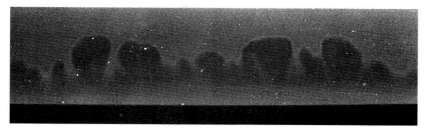

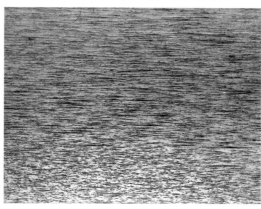

149, 150. *Nugui.*

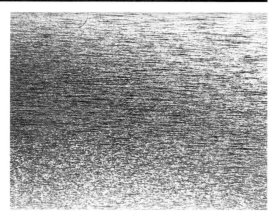

151, 152. *Hadori.*

153. Tools for making the *yokote* and polishing the point: (*a*) bamboo spatula, (*b*) bamboo mask, (*c*) small *hazuya* stone, (*d*) larger *hazuya* stone supported by folded paper on a *narume-dai*.

154. The *yokote* is made by using the spatula to move the *hazuya* along the edge of the mask.

Kissaki no narume: Polishing the Point

As mentioned above, during foundation polishing Fujishiro always moves the point area (the *boshi*) over the polishing stones perpendicular to the length of the blade, even though he polishes the body of the blade at a different angle for each grade of stone he is using. During the first three steps of finish polishing, *hazuya*, *jizuya*, and *nugui*, the point is not touched at all.

The point area is conventionally set off from the rest of the blade by a straight line (called the *yokote*) that runs across the blade from the ridgeline to the edge. The *yokote* may be an actual ridge created by the smith when he is hammering and shaping the blade. Or, in an older sword, the line may be merely a visual demarcation with the real *yokote* ridge long since polished away. In both cases, the area of the sword between the *yokote* and the tip must be polished separately to make it stand out from the rest of the blade.

Where there is no clear *yokote*, Fujishiro has to make one. He begins this during the early polishing stages using the coarser stones. Now he must finish the point and make a clearly visible *yokote* line. To protect the already polished areas, he wraps all of the blade except the point in a cotton cloth. Holding the sword straight up in the air, Fujishiro takes a flat piece of bamboo (the *yokote-kiri*) and positions it on the blade so that its edge is aligned with what will become the *yokote*. Generally, the *yokote* line will meet the edge where it begins to curve up toward the point, and it will form an angle perpendicular not to the ridgeline but to an imaginary line that joins the point and the *machi* on the back of the sword.

Fujishiro, holding the bamboo mask in place with his left hand, now lays the sword on a flat work surface, with the point area extending just a bit past its edge. He wets the point area with *tojiru* and places a small, square piece of *hazuya* flush against the edge of the mask. While holding the *hazuya* in place with a bamboo spatula he moves it back and forth along the mask. When he removes the stone and the *yokote-kiri*, he should see a clear and sharp *yokote*; the portion of the point area adjacent to it that has been polished with the *hazuya* will be much whiter than the rest of the blade surface (very similar to what happened with *hadori*).

To safely finish the rest of the point Fujishiro uses an ingenious device called a *narume-dai*. This is a small, oblong piece of wood (about 1 inch wide by 10 inches long) that has had several latitudinal half-sections removed with a saw to make its top surface flexible and springy. Fujishiro takes soft Japanese paper and folds it until it is as wide as the *narume-dai* and is eight to ten layers thick. He wets the paper thoroughly, places a large thin piece of *hazuya* stone on its top surface, and then lays both paper and stone on top of the *narume-dai*.

The purpose of this tool is to completely support and cushion the *hazuya*. The wooden underpinning is a shock absorber, while the moist paper pillow works a bit like a universal joint, enabling the stone to move easily in any direction according to the pressure the polisher puts on it with the sword. As Fujishiro holds the *narume-dai* in position with his right heel on the *fumaegi*, he moves the point area, from *yokote* to tip, over the *hazuya*, always in a direction perpendicular to the length of the blade. The result will be a *boshi* whose matte finish and white color make it stand out from the rest of the blade.

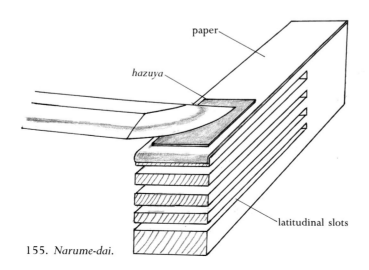

155. *Narume-dai*.

156. Fujishiro polishes the rest of the point on the *narume-dai* until it is a uniform light color with no visible scratches or abrasions.

Migaki: Burnishing

To complete a polishing job, Fujishiro burnishes the *mune*, the back blade, and the *shinogiji*, the surface of the blade between the back and the ridgeline. This creates a decorative contrast between these areas and the rest of the blade. He also polishes the inner surfaces of any grooves.

Burnishing is a process whereby the steel is compacted under pressure to create a bright reflective surface. This is quite different from polishing with stones, where abrading the surface makes the steel details show up as points of scattered light.

The basic technique involved here is quite simple. First Fujishiro cleans the blade carefully to remove all traces of oil and dirt from the surface to be burnished. Then he dusts the blade with a very fine lubricating powder, called *ibota*, derived from the waxy excretion of a cicada-like insect. Holding a steel needle (the *migaki-bo*) like a pencil in his hand, Fujishiro rubs it briskly over the steel surface until an even, mirrorlike finish is obtained. Here and there he applies bamboo masks to prevent the needle from slipping over the ridge or into an unburnished area. Fujishiro uses at least four different shapes of needle.

Finally, after some ten days to two weeks, Fujishiro's job is done. The finished, polished sword will have clean, well-defined lines; a clear and even finish on the steel with a distinct grain, color, and texture; a visible hamon; a properly delineated and finished point; and a pleasing contrast in the upper burnished surfaces. Whatever the blade's individual character or personality, it should now be evident when examined by an expert eye.

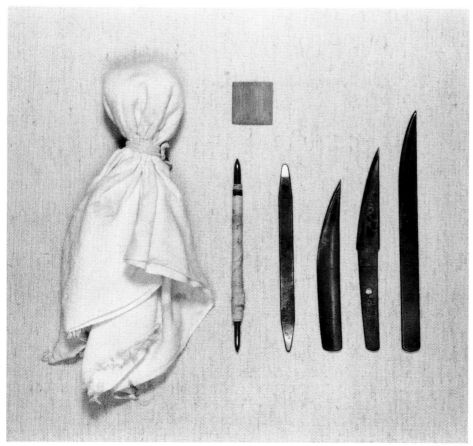

157. Tools used for burnishing: needles, bamboo mask,
and a silk dusting bag filled with *ibota* powder.

158. Fujishiro burnishes the back of the blade with a steel needle.

HIROSHI MIYAJIMA

The Habaki

Appreciation of the Japanese sword demands that its surface finish be smooth and clear to reveal all the details of the steel. This creates a practical problem when it comes to storage. The blade is kept in a scabbard, and if it rubs against the inside walls of this sheath it will eventually scratch. This has not been a concern in the West, where leather or wooden scabbards were made to fit as tightly as needed to secure the blade. The Japanese scabbard, however, had to be made to hold the blade loosely within it, so that the sword would slide in and out only along its burnished back surface.

But the blade must be secured in the scabbard somehow, or it could fall out at any time—an obvious inconvenience. The Japanese solution was to make a habaki, a wedge-shaped collar that fits around the base of the blade against the two notches that mark the beginning of the tang: the *hamachi* on the edge, and the *mune-machi* on the back. The tapered shape of the habaki holds the blade snugly in the scabbard hole, thus allowing the rest of the blade to "float" in the scabbard, its surface barely touched by the wood.

Exactly how the habaki developed in Japan is not known. Like much of sword technology, it may have come from China by way of Korea. All steel swords in Japan, even the oldest straight blades from about the eighth century, have habaki. Early examples are welded onto the hilt and are short compared with the ones seen today.

Habaki were a separate metal fitting by the Heian period. A few extant examples date from this time. The earliest habaki were probably made from iron, and later from pot metal, most of which was copper. Copper remains the metal of choice today because, being very soft, it easily conforms to the shape of the blade without scratching its steel surface. Unlike habaki today, however, these Heian-period habaki do not have foil coverings or decorations, and their sides are very thin and flat. Occasionally, we find a habaki made from solid gold.

Good examples of habaki in a more modern shape and style—that is, with straight sides, sharper corners, and a flat bottom along the edge of the sword—are seen from about the Momoyama period, the oldest such exam-

159. Metal craftsmen at work on sword fittings, as depicted in an Edo-period illustrated book. The man at the top left is checking the fit of a habaki. Note the small forge and bellows.

ple being the work of the smith Umetada. Habaki of gold were especially popular among affluent fiefs, who used them as a means of stockpiling this precious metal in case of war.

The practice of covering the copper habaki with gold or silver foil probably dates from earlier periods, possibly from Muromachi times when there was extensive use of decorative foil on sword mountings. In Edo times, foil was frequently used either as an economy measure or because the only available base metal was an impure pot metal.

The Silversmith

Hiroshi Miyajima (b. 1947) and his oldest brother, Shinjiro, are the third generation in their family to become makers of habaki and other sword fittings. In Japan they are referred to as silversmiths, because the people with their skills originally emerged from the ranks of silver craftsmen. Shinjiro is the oldest son and began working with his father immediately after finishing high school. A second brother in the family has never been interested in the work.

Miyajima was disinclined to follow the family tradition when he was young because he noticed how his father was always at work every day and late into the evening. After he graduated from high school, he went to work at a company that manufactured micrometers. The job demanded considerable handwork, and Miyajima tired of it, deciding that he would be better off self-employed and on his own.

Considering his background, becoming a silversmith seemed a natural route to take. Swords were becoming increasingly popular in Japan, and it appeared that there would be plenty of good opportunities for work. Miyajima had no experience as a silversmith, but from the age of ten he had been

160. Habaki of one-piece copper construction covered in gold foil. This and the following three habaki are by Hiroshi Miyajima.

161. Habaki of one-piece copper construction, with large and small grooves and decorative file marks.

162. Habaki of two-piece copper construction, covered in gold foil with vertical and horizontal file marks.

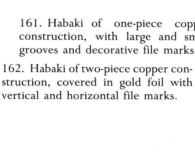

163. Habaki of two-piece construction, with inner piece of polished black *shakudo* and outer piece of copper covered in gold foil with file marks.

delivering swords for his father to clients, and good blades were always in the home. At age twenty-two, Miyajima became his father's apprentice.

Miyajima's first job was repairing sword guards (*tsuba*) and making *seppa*, spacers or washers that fit between the habaki and the guard. He was not allowed to work on habaki yet, because to do this he would have to work too close to the blade, and the risk of chipping or damaging the sword was too high. Later, when he finally did start making habaki, for a year the only ones he was permitted to make were for fencing swords, because here the mistakes of a novice would get lost among the wear and tear these blades endure as a matter of course.

Miyajima's father was not a very strict teacher. According to Miyajima's own testimony he was therefore rather slow to learn. After three years he was able to make single-piece habaki out of copper or silver. After six years he was making two-piece habaki out of copper and gold. When seven years had passed he began making habaki with foil covers.

Had Miyajima concentrated only on habaki, he probably could have completed his training in only four years. But because he was intent on also learning how to make sword fittings for *koshirae*—*fuchi* and *kashira* (the collars at both ends of the hilt), *menuki* (grip ornaments), *seppa*, and handles for the ac-

164. Ichiro Miyajima shows his son Hiroshi a Heian-style *koshirae* that he made for a sword by Yoshindo.

companying tools and utility knives (*kogai* and *kozuka*)—it took him eight years in all before he was ready to become an independent craftsman. His first commission—in 1976—was from Yoshindo, who has since become a regular client. Miyajima feels his work has improved over the years in large part because of Yoshindo's demanding nature.

Today Miyajima lives east of Tokyo, just beyond the Edogawa River. His house is so small there is no room to work in it, so every day he travels to the home of his father in the nearby city of Chiba. His father, in turn, obligingly makes room for him there by traveling every day into Tokyo to work at his son Shinjiro.

Miyajima makes about a hundred habaki a year. Only a small amount of his yearly output involves other kinds of scabbard fittings like *fuchi, kashira,* and *menuki*. He is occasionally, for example, asked to repair fittings or make missing fittings to match an existing old *koshirae*. *Koshirae* are demanding in that all the parts of the sword and its scabbard must be considered as an artistic whole. Miyajima would like to double the amount of work he does on *koshirae*, but at the moment he can't since he relies on the habaki work for the bulk of his income. He envies his father and brother who, being older and more established (Miyajima's father, after five decades at work, is one of the most esteemed silversmiths in Japan today), are able to spend well over half their time on more elaborate projects.

The metals most commonly used for habaki and other sword fittings are copper, gold, silver, and, rarely, *shakudo*. *Shakudo* is an old Japanese alloy of roughly 96 percent copper and 4 percent gold. It looks and works like copper, but oxidizes to a beautiful black finish. Sometimes brass is used, Japanese brass being softer than the typical variety found in the United States.

The kind of metal Miyajima uses for a particular job depends on the sword, but he prefers gold, which is easy to work and very appealing to the eye. When doing repair work, he must be careful that the finish of the new metal matches that of the other fittings on the *koshirae*. Once, Miyajima was asked to make a new habaki for a sword to which there was already a very old *koshirae*, with copper fittings of a curious greenish color. To match this copper Miyajima had to obtain a special shipment of 350-year-old tiles that had been removed from the roof of Japan's famous Nikko Shrine. Frequently, Miyajima has to use chemicals to get the exact finish he needs.

A basic habaki, one consisting of a single piece of copper, costs about $150 and can be made in a day. Adding gold foil will double the price and the time to make it. A two-piece gold habaki—which is always what Yoshindo requests—will cost almost $450. Generally clients specify only the materials, the budget, and the kind of construction (one- or two-piece). Miyajima decides the rest, basing his design on the shape and character of the sword.

Miyajima feels that contemporary swords are easier to work on than antique swords. On some old swords, due to years of polishing and sharpening the edge, the blade is thinner than the tang and the *hamachi* is almost gone. This makes it very hard to get a good fit. He also feels that modern habaki are in some respects more attractive than older ones, which have had their lines blurred and their corners rounded off from excessive handling. Some habaki makers erroneously copy these soft shapes, thinking they are traditional when they are simply the result of many years of wear. Miyajima believes that the more square and angular habaki being made today are probably closer to the classical ideal.

Miyajima once enjoyed fishing and photography, but now his main recreation is sitting around relaxing, drinking and talking with his friends. He works from nine in the morning to six at night, seven days a week, only taking time off over the New Year's holiday or to meet with clients. In the evening he is often out delivering his work to his customers.

Today in Japan there are probably about fifty active habaki makers. Most of these silversmiths make fittings for *koshirae* as well. Every year the NBTHK has a special contest for habaki. Miyajima finished first four years in a row, from 1981 to 1984, and again in 1986. Only one habaki maker, Nobuo Asai, has been elevated to *mukansa*.

THE CRAFT

The most important aesthetic feature of a habaki is its shape. In height it is generally 80 percent of the width of the blade, measured at the *machi* just above the tang. For a small dagger the height of the habaki will be 60–70 percent of the width of the blade. An older, thin sword will require a different proportion for the blade to look good.

In all cases, however, the proportions of an individual habaki must be designed to be visually pleasing and to complement the shape of the blade. Other considerations are (1) that the front (along the edge or *ha* of the blade) be a straight line; (2) that the back (along the back ridge or *mune*) be slightly concave to follow the curvature of the blade; (3) that the sides be flat and straight; and (4) that the widest one-third of the habaki be along its bottom (toward the tang) where it contacts the scabbard.

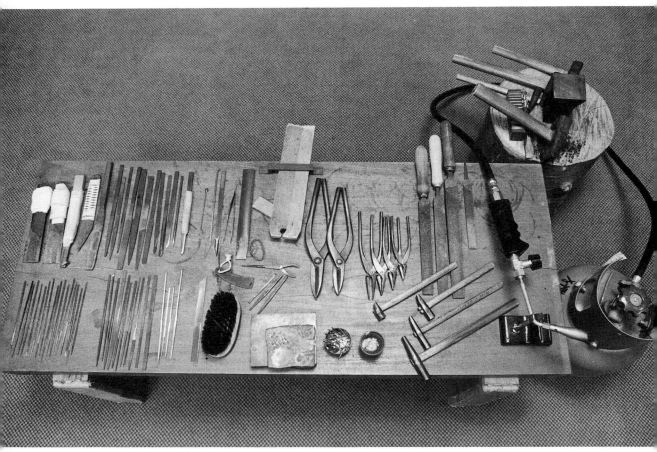

165. Miyajima's tools: propane torch, pliers, various
small hammers and files, burnishing needles.

Miyajima's tools consist primarily of different-sized hammers and files.
The hammers are used to shape the blank in the early stages of forging. As
the copper is hammered, bent, and fitted it becomes compacted and less
malleable; this is called work hardening. To make it malleable again, Miyajima must periodically heat it until it is red hot and then cool it by dipping it
in water (like *yaki-ire* but with the opposite effect; only steel is hardened by
heating and quenching). Miyajima uses a propane torch to heat the copper;
in the past, silversmiths kept a small bellows and forge in their workshops.

The habaki shown being made in this chapter is the most common type
seen today; it uses a single piece of copper covered in a gold-foil jacket.
Two-piece habaki are made for larger swords when more support is
necessary. These have an outer forged jacket that fits over an inner notched
sleeve.

Jiganedori: Cutting the Blank

Miyajima takes a sheet of copper a bit more than an eighth of an inch thick. Using a chisel, he cuts out a rectangular piece 2 inches long by 1 inch wide. This starting piece, or blank, is slightly larger than the final piece he will need to allow for stock removal by hammering and filing. Its thickness must match exactly the depth of the *mune-machi*, the notch that delineates the back of the blade from the tang and that will support the habaki when it is in place.

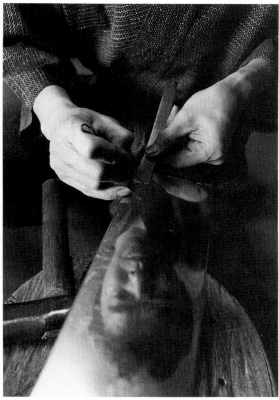

166. Miyajima marks out the piece of copper he will use for the habaki.

167. The blank is cut out with a chisel.

Hizukuri: Forging

Miyajima uses a small hammer with a wedge-shaped head to work and form the copper. He hammers along the width of the blank so that it gradually tapers in thickness across its surface, from a bit less (toward the point) to a bit more (toward the tang) than an eighth of an inch. It is this variation in thickness that will enable the habaki to wedge snugly inside the scabbard mouth and hold the sword in place. With a hacksaw Miyajima cuts out a notch in the center of the blank where it will fit around the *mune-machi*. He cuts the notch a bit smaller than needed to allow for later fitting by filing and folding.

168. The finished blank: one edge is thicker than the other.

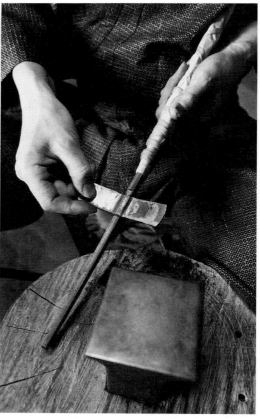

169. Miyajima checks the fit of the habaki on the sword.

170. A square notch is removed to fit around the *mune-machi*.

Ouimage and Toshin-awase: Fitting around the Blade

Miyajima lays the flat blank across a U-shaped mold and punches it into the cavity to begin bending its sides upward to fit around the blade. Then, firmly holding the sword (which has been wrapped in paper to protect its polished surface) against his wooden workbench, he hammers the habaki blank onto the blade, working gradually from the back to the front. The notch in the center of the blank should now fit neatly around the *mune-machi*.

Miyajima continues hammering until the habaki fits firmly and snugly on both sides of the blade and along the back. The inner surface of the habaki must conform exactly to the contours of the steel to prevent slipping or shifting on the sword. The back of the habaki is closed firmly against the *mune-machi*. Using a file and a saw, Miyajima trims the excess along the open front of the habaki, evening the edges so that they both extend slightly past the *hamachi*.

171. Miyajima hammers the habaki to shape it exactly to the blade.

172. The fit and proportions of the habaki are checked against the blade.

Hamachi-ire: Sealing the Habaki

The narrow gap on the front of the habaki is now sealed using a small triangular wedge of copper called the *machigane*. When in place inside the habaki, the *machigane* will be slightly recessed from the top edge (toward the point) so as to support the habaki against the *hamachi*. It tapers to fit exactly into the narrow gap along the habaki's front edge and then broadens to the thickness of the tang to provide maximum support along the blade.

Miyajima cuts the blank for the *machigane* out of a piece of copper, leaving a bit of a tail on it to make it easier to hold in his fingers as he files and shapes it. When it is ready, he wedges the *machigane* into place inside the habaki. Then, holding the entire assembly up to a torch, Miyajima heats it until it turns a dull red. When he inserts a sliver of solid silver solder into the hot habaki, the solder melts and flows around the *machigane*, thus completing the seal. The fit of the habaki may now have to be slightly adjusted to the blade again.

173. The *machigane* is ready to be fitted into the habaki.

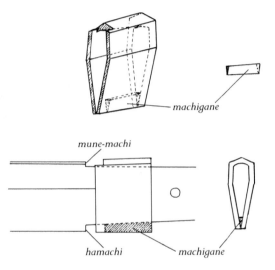

174. The *machigane* supports the blade along the front edge of the tang.

175. Soldering holds the *machigane* in place and also seals the habaki shut.

176. The soldered habaki is again fitted and adjusted to the blade.

Yasurigake: Filing

Miyajima can now file the closed and fitted habaki into the proper shape. This involves squaring all the lines and giving the sides a smooth finish. For this he uses not polishing stones but a series of three flat files that get progressively finer as the copper surface gets smoother. The curvature of the front and back edges of the habaki is for the most part determined by the respective shapes of the edge and back of the blade. The shape of the top edge of the habaki will vary depending on Miyajima's overall design for the piece. The bottom edge will be made flat to fit snugly against the hilt.

Miyajima could stop here if he chose to, finishing the piece by filing or cutting decorative grooves into the copper to form fence patterns, geometrical designs, flowers, or other motifs. The most common pattern seen on a bare habaki is rows of diagonal marks along the bottom two-thirds of the body. Miyajima must be careful not to make his filing too rough, or the habaki will soon wear out the scabbard mouth.

But since Miyajima is planning a jacket for the habaki we have been describing, at this stage he simply makes sure that the shape of the habaki is what he wants, and that its surface is completely smooth and filed down enough to allow for the application of foil.

177. Filing smooths the edges and straightens the lines.

178. The habaki is ready for finishing.

Kisegane-awase: Fitting the Decorative Foil

Miyajima measures the habaki for its jacket by wrapping it in a piece of paper. He then lays this paper over the flat gold or silver foil sheet to serve as a template or cutting guide. The piece of foil he obtains will have a width slightly greater than the height of the habaki, and a length equal to that of the habaki's total circumference.

The silver foil Miyajima uses is about 0.008 inch (0.2 mm) thick and 99 percent pure. The gold foil he usually uses ranges from 0.0055 inch (0.14 mm) to 0.008 inch in thickness, but can be as thick as 0.01 inch (0.3 mm) if it is going to be engraved. Miyajima prefers an 18-karat gold mixed with silver. This makes the gold suitably flexible for habaki making. However, silver also gives the gold a slightly blue dullish tinge that must later be removed with chemicals.

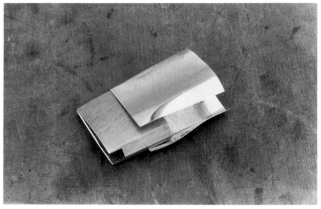

179. Gold foil is cut to fit around the habaki.

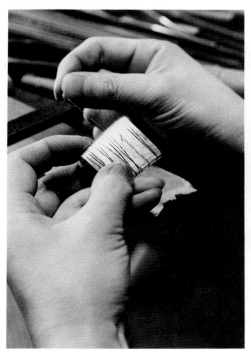

180, 181. The jacket is tied with wire thread and soldered shut.

Miyajima takes the piece of foil and wraps it over the habaki, creasing it to give it a permanent fold. The two ends of the foil that touch along the center line on the back of the habaki must now be soldered shut. Miyajima removes the foil envelope from the habaki and, being careful not to distort its shape, wraps iron thread around and around it until the seam is bound completely along its length. He then holds the foil up to a torch. When it is just getting hot, he touches a strand of solid gold solder to the length of the seam from the inside. The solder melts, flows into the gap, and seals the foil up tight.

Like the habaki, the jacket is wedge shaped, the wider end being on the bottom toward the tang. Miyajima therefore begins slipping the jacket on over the narrower top of the habaki. He pulls it down until it is snug and won't go any further; this is usually at a point about halfway down the side of the habaki. If the foil were to slip easily all the way over the habaki it would mean that it was too loose. Eventually, the constant back and forth friction caused by taking the sword in and out of the scabbard would tear the foil off completely.

To get the jacket to go the rest of the way down the habaki, Miyajima starts making file marks along the surface of the foil. These will ultimately become part of the habaki's surface decoration. Here, though, they have a practical function. The tiny filed grooves in the foil can be pulled apart and opened to allow the jacket to stretch out and down.

After he has filed about a half an inch of the foil surface, Miyajima holds the top of the jacket and very gently taps up on the base of the habaki with a small hammer. This drives the habaki further into the jacket. But not all the way. Miyajima files on the foil for another half-inch or so. Then he taps the base of the habaki again. In this way, the foil is gradually filed and stretched until the jacket completely covers the habaki.

182. Filing is done for decoration and to enable the foil jacket to stretch over the habaki. Here the jacket is almost completely in place.

Vertical File Marks

Horizontal File Marks

Slanting File Marks

Cross-hatched

Filed with Burrs (*Yujo*)

Full Chiseled Burrs

Rounded Burrs

Koke ("Moss")

Polished

183. Common habaki surface designs.

184. Miyajima uses a burnishing needle to bend the edge of the foil over the bottom of the habaki.

185. The foil surface must often be chemically treated to obtain the color and finish that Miyajima wants.

There should now be a bit of foil extending out over the top and bottom edges of the habaki. Miyajima folds these loose ends down, completely covering all the visible copper to secure the foil from being pulled in a vertical direction. No glue or paste of any kind is used to hold the foil in place.

The file marks, in addition to making the habaki more attractive—silversmiths use an astonishing range of decorative patterns—also improve the grip of the scabbard mouth on the habaki by roughening the foil surface. The file marks can be very fine or very coarse, or a mixture of these depending on the desired effect. One common technique is to push the file and then halt suddenly without following through on the stroke. This leaves tiny burrs or spikes inside the file marks that add considerably to the texture of the final motif.

Most of the files Miyajima uses for this kind of decorative work are actually modified saw blades. The size of their teeth varies. Small-toothed saws work best on curved surfaces, while saws with larger teeth work best on broad, flat surfaces. Miyajima makes these files himself from hacksaw blades. He removes any offset teeth and files in new ones that will leave only a single mark per stroke.

When the jacket is finally filed and in place, Miyajima cleans its surfaces with soap, charcoal, and sometimes chemicals. In the process called *iroage*, he uses the following mixture of chemicals to restore the glint to the gold whose silver content has made it a dullish blue: 1 part *kunroku* (a kind of pine resin frequently used in herbal medicines), 4.5 parts rock salt, 4.5 parts potassium nitrate, 3.5 parts copper sulfate, and 2 parts ferric sulfate. He brushes this solution onto the habaki and then heats it to make the chemicals react. When the habaki cools, he washes it with water. After *iroage* is repeated several times, the surface of the habaki will be bright and slightly tinged with red.

The Scabbard

A polished Japanese sword needs a properly fitted scabbard to preserve and protect it. A fully mounted Japanese scabbard, or *koshirae*, will generally have a lacquered body, a taped hilt, a sword guard, a utility knife, and other small implements and decorative metal fittings. *Koshirae* can be very elaborate, and indeed tended to be so when the sword as a weapon became less important in Edo times. Today, however, most new swords are mounted for storage in a less expensive type of scabbard made of plain, unfinished wood: the *shira-zaya*, or "white scabbard."

The exterior of the plain wooden scabbard differs greatly from its more decorative lacquered cousin, which was intended for actual use and display. Inside, however, the requirements of each are the same. As mentioned in the previous chapter, the scabbard is made so that the blade slides into or out of it on its burnished back surface only; if the scabbard were to rub against the sides of the blade, its polished metal surface would scratch and become clouded. The blade is secured in the scabbard only by the pressure of the scabbard mouth around the habaki. Yet the blade cannot "rattle" within the scabbard either. Fitting the wood to the sword is the special art of the scabbard maker.

Throughout most of Japanese history, swords have customarily been kept in full *koshirae*. A single sword might have several different mountings, each one appropriate to a particular season or occasion. Plain wooden scabbards have been found from the early Edo period, when they were used for the safekeeping of swords donated to shrines. These early *shira-zaya* were crudely made, and were oval or eight-sided in cross-section.

In the later Edo period, some wealthy samurai who wore full mountings when they took their swords outside would replace them with plain wooden scabbards for storage at home. These storage scabbards were called *yasume-zaya* ("resting scabbards") or *abura-zaya* ("oil scabbards"). After 1876, when the new Meiji government proscribed the wearing of swords, the importance of full mountings declined. For a sword that could not be carried about in public, a plain wrapper was sufficient. Only in recent times have full *koshirae* come back into fashion in Japan—although it is still illegal to carry a sword about.

The Woodcarver

The family of Kazuyuki Takayama (b. 1940) has been making scabbards for about 150 years over six generations. The first two generations of the family worked in Hamamatsu, near the city of Nagoya; the third generation moved to Tokyo, where the family now resides.

Takayama's father began making scabbards at the age of twelve. At first Kazuyuki wanted to be a polisher and spent several years studying with the Fujishiro family. He continued his polishing work even while attending college and then while working at a company. He dreamed of becoming a polisher full time.

But at the age of twenty-five, after everyone kept telling him that because of his family history his destiny lay with scabbards, Takayama became his father's student. The years spent polishing, however, were not wasted. They taught him to examine sword blades, and to understand their subtle contours and the kind of damage that results when a scabbard is poorly made.

Five years after joining his father, Takayama became an independent scabbard maker. In the beginning he was so slow and had to work so carefully to do a good job that he lost money on his scabbard business and had to supplement his work with polishing jobs. While he has today mastered his techniques—he is the only *mukansa*-level scabbard maker in Japan and is a judge at the annual NBTHK contest for scabbard makers and metal craftsmen—he remains a deliberate perfectionist who works much more slowly than his colleagues. It usually takes him two days to finish a plain wooden scabbard. Making a full *koshirae* may take him half a year.

About half the swords that come to Takayama are completely polished; usually these are older swords that need replacement scabbards. The other swords Takayama gets are new swords that, having been polished up to the *kaisei* stage, are being fitted for a scabbard for the first time. The habaki will already be on the new blade. When Takayama is done he will send the sword on to the polisher for finishing.

186. Takayama's shop. The workbench is a quilt-covered log.

187. A wood shaving showing Takayama's precise and even control over the chisel.

Most of Takayama's commissions are for plain wooden scabbards, which he sells for about $300; a smaller number are for full *koshirae*, which may cost $6,000 or more. When brought a fully mounted sword and asked to make a replacement scabbard, he must match his work to the metal fittings and other pieces of the *koshirae* that still exist. Commissions from museums often demand that he replicate old styles. Making *koshirae* for new swords is what Takayama enjoys most, however, as it gives him a chance to try out his own designs. Occasionally he is asked not only to design the scabbard but to supervise the making of the other fittings; these he subcontracts out to other specialists.

Takayama's shop is in Nakameguro, western Tokyo. Its total floor area is about 250 square feet. Currently it occupies a room in his house, but he would move it outside if he had more space (this being the standard complaint in Japan). His only requirement for the shop is that it be easy to clean up; woodworking in Japan produces shavings, not sawdust, so the job is relatively easy.

Takayama has one live-in apprentice. When training a new student, Takayama begins by teaching him how to sharpen and maintain the chisels and planes. Over and over again he makes him do the job until he gets it right. Some measure of the importance of these tools and the skill needed to maintain them properly is that Takayama is generally not satisfied with a student's sharpening until he has been at it six months or more.

The cutting edges of Japanese chisels and planes are made of two pieces of hard and soft steel laminated together. The chisels (*nomi*) that Takayama uses to hollow out the scabbard are slightly different from chisels used by other woodworkers in Japan. They have curved shafts to allow them to easily cut below the surface of the wood. They also have rounded tips, which make it easier to control the depth of the stroke and help prevent gouges in the wood. Takayama's woodplanes (*kanna*) require frequent adjusting to make sure that the depth of the cut is right and that the blade is stable in its wooden block. Like other traditional Japanese woodworkers, Takayama does not use sandpaper but planes his wood to a smooth, natural luster. Some of his tools Takayama received from his father; others he has had custom made by blacksmiths (some craftsmen in Japan will put newly made tools in storage for several years before using them in the belief that this "seasons" and improves them). Takayama spends at least an hour every day on sharpening and maintenance. With proper care his tools will last several decades of constant use.

After learning how to sharpen tools, Takayama's students spend their next two years practicing cutting scabbard blanks from scrap wood. Takayama watches them constantly as they work. Like other teachers in Japan, Takayama believes that anything his students do is a direct reflection of his own abilities, and therefore is hesitant to release any student from an apprenticeship before he feels he has become a competent craftsman. This may take as long as ten years.

Like the other craftsmen in this book, Takayama works from morning to night. He rarely takes Sunday off, but since he must attend meetings, talk to customers, and pick up or deliver swords, he is actually in his shop only twenty days a month. For relaxation he goes fishing about four times a year, spending a great deal of time beforehand preparing his fishing gear and planning his expeditions.

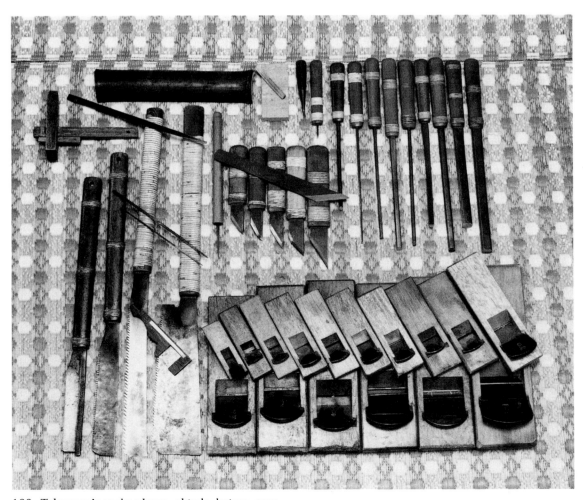

188. Takayama's tools: planes, chisels, knives, saws.

189. Takayama spends at least an hour each day sharpening his tools.

THE CRAFT

Scabbards in Japan are always made of wood from the *ho* tree (*Magnolia obovata* Thunb.). This has been true since at least the Heian period, although examples have also been found in early Japanese tombs. The *ho* tree, which grows all over Japan, is ideal for scabbard making for several reasons. It is soft and will not scratch the blade. It has a regular grain and is easily worked with a plane and chisel. When seasoned properly, *ho* wood has virtually no sap left in it; a dry environment is best suited to protecting and preserving a steel weapon.

The effects of temperature and humidity changes on the wood are a real challenge for the scabbard maker, for they affect the size of the wood and the fit of the blade. Takayama has to make sure that the environment of his work area is similar in humidity and ventilation to that of the area the sword is going to. This was less of a problem thirty years ago because there was much more natural ventilation in Japanese homes. Today, the use of air conditioners and heaters means that homes in a single climatic zone can have widely varying ambient conditions.

Sometimes all Takayama can do is try to compensate at the design stage. For a blade that is going to a drier climate than humid Tokyo's, for example, the fit of the scabbard must be made very loose, almost to the point that the blade falls out by itself. Once the scabbard reaches its destination, the much lower humidity there will cause the wood to shrink, resulting in a perfect fit.

A good scabbard must satisfy several criteria. Most important of these is that the fit of the scabbard be exact, tailored to the individual sword. The seams must be tight to keep out dirt and moisture. The seams must also be strong, yet able to be easily popped apart for occasional cleaning of the interior. The outside should be cleanly manufactured and comfortable to hold. The design of the scabbard should also reflect something of the nature of the sword it contains and protects.

Kidori: Cutting the Blank

Takayama purchases the *ho* wood for his scabbards from shops that specialize in this kind of lumber. He always selects his wood personally, and then has it shipped to his home, where he seasons it in an open-air shed. In about ten years the wood is ready to use.

When Takayama receives an order for a scabbard his first step is to select which piece of *ho* wood he will make it from. He goes to his shed and examines his lumber for color, quality, and thickness—all of which will vary depending on the demands of the sword and the desires of the client. Takayama then takes the piece of wood he has chosen and, working along the grain with a handsaw, cuts it into a rough oblong that has the proper length and width and curvature to accommodate the sword. If he discovers any knots while working—now or later—he will have to discard the wood and start over.

190. The wood for a scabbard is selected from a seasoned batch of *ho* wood.

191. The section of wood that will become the scabbard is marked out on the slab for cutting.

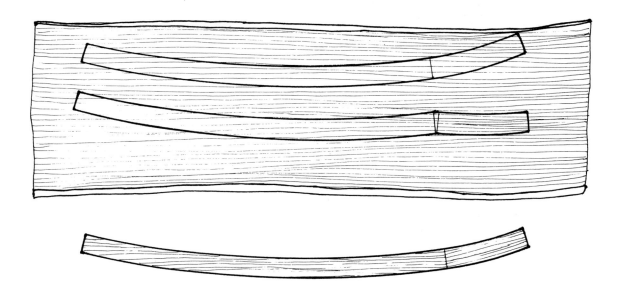

192. When the blade has a large curvature, a wedge-shaped area can be taken out of the blank to "bend" the grain at the junction between the hilt and scabbard.

Nakadoshi: Splitting the Blank

Takayama does not make the scabbard out of two separate pieces of wood. Rather, he takes a single piece, saws it in half, hollows out a groove for the sword, and then fits the two halves back together. He begins by taking the oblong scabbard blank and drawing a line along the center of the surface to be sawn. Then he draws another line along the center of the surface on the opposite side.

Takayama's "workbench" is a section of log about 15 inches in diameter. To cut the blank, Takayama stands on the log and places the blank between his feet, its end extending out over the edge. Bracing the blank with his toes and insteps, Takayama controls his saw with both hands and begins cutting the blank from one end along the line he has drawn. After two or three strokes he rotates the blank 180° and saws along the guideline on the opposite side. After two or three strokes he turns the blank over again. Sawing proceeds in this way until the blank has been cut into two even halves exactly down the center.

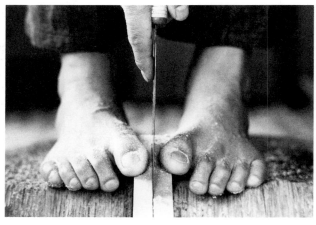

193, 194. The scabbard blank is cut in half.

Mentori: Rough Planing the Exterior

Takayama takes a 2½-inch plane and rounds off all the exterior corners and edges on each half of the scabbard blank to give the wood a smooth, even shape. Japanese woodplanes, like Japanese saws, work on the pulling stroke rather than the pushing stroke. By placing the scabbard blank on a flat board with a raised stop at one end, Takayama can hold the blank steady against his workbench with one hand as he uses his other hand to hold the plane. No clamps are needed.

Takayama next uses a saw to remove the parts of the scabbard halves that will become the hilt.

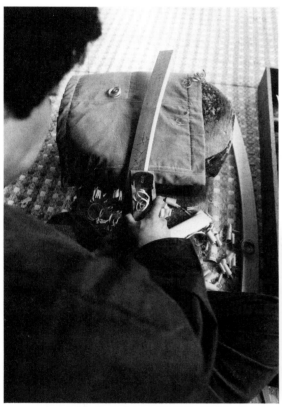

195. Takayama rounds off the outside of the cut scabbard blank with a large plane.

196. The inner surface of each scabbard half is planed until it is flat and smooth. The outer surface remains rounded.

Kezuri-awase: Planing the Inner Surface

Takayama now begins to plane the inner surfaces of the scabbard halves. His goal is to make them perfectly flat so that they can later be glued back together with no gaps or separations anywhere along the seam. When he is done, he places the sword along one of the inside surfaces of the scabbard and traces its outline with a pencil. He repeats this on the inside surface of the other half, making sure that the back of the blade is aligned on the wood here just as it was on the first half.

197. The sections of the blank that will form the hilt have been removed. The sword is kept in a rack to prevent scratches.

198, 199. Guidelines are drawn on the inner surfaces before chiseling.

Kaki-ire: Chiseling out the Space for the Blade

Takayama now hollows out a space to contain the blade in the scabbard by using a series of chisels within the borders of the pencil lines he has drawn. He starts with a quarter-inch chisel. Holding it perpendicular to the wood surface, he cuts a vertical groove along the section of the line that marks the back (*mune*) of the blade. Now, holding the same chisel flat along the wood surface, Takayama begins to carve out a shallow depression along the line of the vertical groove.

Next, using a half-inch chisel, he works along this depression to widen it from the *mune* line toward the edge. Finally he uses a three-quarter-inch chisel to bring the depression all the way to the line marking the edge of the blade. Using these three chisels in sequence produces a hollow on the scabbard half that accommodates half the volume of the blade and that is deepest on the *mune* side but very shallow on the edge side.

200. The chiseling is about half finished. The space for the edge of the sword is to the left.

201. The fit of the blade in the scabbard half needs frequent checking.

Takayama now repeats this carving sequence on the inside surface of the other scabbard half. The scabbard halves are now identical in every respect but two. First, the carved-out area on one half will be made with a shallow lip to protect the edge of the blade, while the corresponding area on the other scabbard half will gradually taper out and flatten. This prevents the blade from resting directly on the glued seam of the scabbard when the halves are put together. Second, on one of the scabbard halves, below the area where the point will rest, there will be a shallow pocket to collect any excess oil on the blade that drains off during storage.

Takayama next uses a thick-handled stubby knife called a *yokogaki* to scrape and clean the inner surface of the scabbard crosswise against the grain. Then he carves out the part of the scabbard mouth that will be in contact with the habaki. He must make it just wide enough to grip the habaki when it is about two-thirds of the way in. If the habaki itself has not been perfectly fitted to the blade, it is almost impossible for the scabbard maker to perform this crucial step correctly.

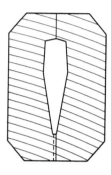

202. One half of the scabbard is given a shallow lip to contain the edge of the blade.

203. The pocket below the point area collects drainage from the oiled and polished blade.

204. The hollow in the scabbard is finished and smoothed with a knife.

A similar procedure is followed for the two halves of the hilt: a section is carved out to receive the tang of the sword.

Takayama now rubs the inside surface of the scabbard with a piece of *tokusa*, or horsetail reed (*Equisetum hyemale*), an ornamental evergreen popular in Japanese gardens and also used by woodworkers for its mild abrasive qualities. Real sandpaper is never used; not only would it destroy the luster of the wood, but, in the case of a scabbard, it might leave a piece of grit behind that would scratch a sword blade.

Takayama can now check the fit of the scabbard by tying its two halves tightly together with a cord. He coats the sword with clove oil and inserts it briefly into the scabbard. He then removes the cord, opens the scabbard, and examines its internal surfaces for oil stains. Stains indicate that parts of the blade are rubbing against the wood. These areas can be trimmed or adjusted with a knife or chisel until there is a proper fit.

Norizuke: Gluing

Now that Takayama has checked to make sure that all the internal surfaces are true, that there are no gaps or separations anywhere, and that the depression for the sword is precisely fitted to the blade, he is ready to glue the scabbard halves together. For glue, he uses one- or two-day-old cooked rice. Rice glue (called *sokui*) is used here because it does not draw moisture and is strong, but not so strong that it prevents the scabbard from being sprung open along its seams for cleaning. Takayama works the rice against a flat piece of wood with a bamboo spatula, now and then adding tiny dabs of water. In a few minutes, the rice becomes a sticky, glutinous paste.

205, 206. The scabbard halves are glued together with cooked rice that has been worked into a paste with a spatula.

207. Glue is applied only to the outer edges of the scabbard halves.

208. Takayama ties the glued scabbard halves together.

Takayama uses a small spatula to run a thin bead of rice glue along the outside edges of the scabbard halves. Then, wrapping one end of a long cord around the scabbard, he puts the other end of the cord in his mouth. It is said that scabbard makers need strong teeth, and the reason for this is apparent now. In order to wind the rope tightly and uniformly along the entire length of the scabbard, he has to clamp the binding cord in his mouth as he pushes firmly on the scabbard and rapidly twists it in both his hands.

Takayama places the bound scabbard aside to let it set overnight, and then glues the two halves of the hilt together the same way.

Arakezuri: Rough Planing the Cut Surface

After the glue has set, Takayama begins planing and shaping the outside surface. He begins with the area around the scabbard mouth and, using a knife, creates the final shape of the scabbard in cross-section.

It is at this point that Takayama decides exactly what the scabbard will look like, its height in relation to its width, its thickness relative to the sword, the configuration of its surface. A popular scabbard style today calls for an octagonal cross-section; this is what is shown in the photographs here. The scabbard maker must decide how sharply to define the ridges between the eight surfaces, and he must be sure that the strength of each ridge does not vary along the entire length of the wood. Other scabbards may be smooth and oval in cross-section.

209. The outline of the scabbard is cut around the mouth with a knife to serve as a guide for the rest of the planing.

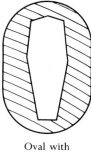

Oval with
Flat Sides

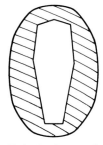

Eight Surfaces with
Rounded Ridges

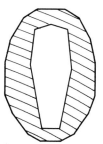

Eight Surfaces with
Beveled Ridges

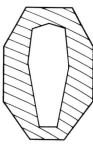

Eight Surfaces with
Sharp Ridges

Oval

210. Scabbard designs.

211. The exterior of the scabbard is roughly shaped with a plane.

Some scabbard makers use the same scabbard design time and time again, regardless of the shape of the blade within. Takayama's scabbards are all unique, each one aptly conveying something of the nature of the sword it was made for. An older, thin blade, for example, will have a much slenderer scabbard than a robust modern blade. The curvature of the blade will also match the grain of the wood as closely as possible.

Takayama inserts the blade, which has also been inserted into the hilt. Now, using a large, coarse plane, he works the surface of the scabbard until it conforms to the outline he has carved around the scabbard mouth. From this stage on the blade is mostly kept in the scabbard, and the scabbard and the hilt are planed and shaped and finished as a single unit.

Nakakezuri: Fine Planing the Outside

After rough planing, Takayama goes over the entire outer surface of the scabbard and hilt with a finer plane. All eight wooden surfaces should be clearly visible now, clean and smooth. Takayama must be especially careful at this stage not to cross over and dull any of the ridges along the length of the scabbard. Finally, Takayama uses a plane on the surfaces around the mouths of the scabbard and the hilt so that they will join evenly.

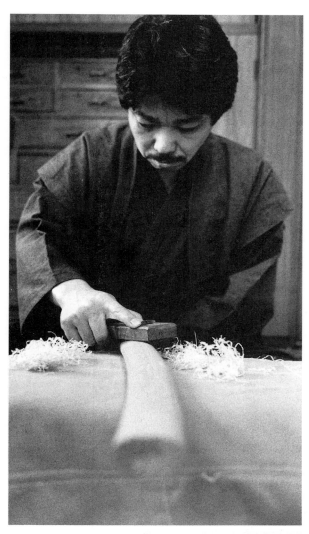

212. As the work proceeds, the planes grow smaller and smaller. Note the fine shavings.

213. The top is also planed so that scabbard and hilt meet on a perfectly flat surface.

Mekugi-ana-ake: Drilling the Rivet Hole

The blade is held in the hilt by a bamboo rivet called a *mekugi*, which passes through a hole (the *mekugi-ana*) that the swordsmith has drilled in the metal tang. With the blade held snugly in the scabbard by the habaki, Takayama lays the hilt of the scabbard against the tang, in a position corresponding to where it will be when the sword is finally mounted. The hole in the tang tells him where the hole in the hilt has to be. After marking the spot, Takayama takes an awl and drills through the soft wood of the hilt. The hole must be tapered, with its diameter larger on one side of the hilt than the other. This will allow the rivet to be wedged firmly into place. Takayama cleans the hole and corrects its taper with a small drill or file.

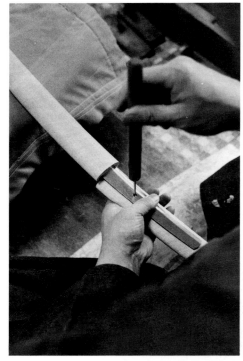

214, 215. Using the sword tang as a guide, Takayama marks and drills the rivet hole (*mekugi-ana*) into the hilt.

Shiagekezuri: Finish Planing

Using very small planes, only an inch or so wide, Takayama goes over all the surfaces of the scabbard one last time. He is now handling the scabbard with white cotton gloves and has draped a thick cloth over the workbench. *Ho* wood is soft to begin with, and it is now so finely finished that the least bit of dust or shavings accidentally rubbed on its surface will make a very visible scratch.

Takayama next uses his knife to bevel the edges of the scabbard at top and bottom. This makes the scabbard more pleasant to look at and comfortable to touch, and also eliminates sharp corners that might easily bruise.

Fukurohari: Wrapping the Scabbard in Paper

A paper wrapping is used to protect the scabbard until it reaches its new home. Usually this paper is a rough-textured stock called *nishi no uchi*, after the name of the place in Ibaraki Prefecture where it is made. *Nishi no uchi* is very durable, and is also used to make oil papers such as those found on Japanese umbrellas.

Takayama takes a strip of paper and, while pulling on it slightly to stretch it, wraps it in a spiral around the entire length of the scabbard. He spreads a thin line of glue along the edge of the paper as it is wrapped to secure it in place. The paper wrapping should conform exactly to the shape of the scabbard. It can be removed by simply lifting it off like a slipcover.

216. Paper is wrapped and glued around the scabbard to make a protective jacket.

Shiagemigaki: Finish Polishing

The wood surface of the scabbard is polished to complete the job. Takayama removes the paper from the scabbard. Then he goes over the entire scabbard with a sanding block he has made from pieces of *tokusa* that have been boiled, cut open into flat strips, and then glued onto a block of wood (about 2 inches by 4 inches). The abrasive action here is much milder than even the finest grade of sandpaper.

Takayama goes over the scabbard once more, this time with a used *tokusa* sanding block (one that has already been used on four or five scabbards) and a light coating of *ibota*, the insect-derived powder already mentioned in connection with polishing. This gives the wood a glossy, polished, and finished appearance, as if it had been carefully waxed.

Takayama now slips the scabbard back into its paper wrapping for delivery to its owner or to send on to the swordsmith or polisher.

217, 218. The wood surface is dusted with *ibota* powder and then given a final polish with a piece of horsetail reed (*tokusa*) on a sanding block.

Bibliography

Compton, Walter A., et al. *Nippon-to: Art Swords of Japan.* New York: Japan Society, 1976.

Dobrée, Alfred. *Japanese Sword Blades.* London: Arms and Armour Press, 1967.

Fukunaga, Suiken. *Katana kaji no seikatsu* [in Japanese]. Tokyo: Yuzankaku Shuppan, 1969.

Hakusui, Inami. *Nippon-to: The Japanese Sword.* Tokyo: Japan Sword Co., 1948.

Harris, Victor. "Japanese Swords and the Bizen Tradition." *Arts of Asia,* May/June 1986, pp. 125–29.

Hickman, B., ed. *Japanese Crafts, Materials and Their Applications.* London: East-West Publications, 1977.

Joly, Henri, and Hagitaro Inada. *The Sword and Samé.* London: Holland Press, 1962.

Miyairi, Akihira, et al. *Nippon-to no dekiru made* [in Japanese]. Vol. 7 of *Nippon-to zenshu.* Tokyo: Tokuma Shoten, 1966.

Nitobe, Inazo. *Bushido: The Soul of Japan.* 1905. Reprint. Tokyo: Charles E. Tuttle, 1969.

Ogasawara, Nobuo. *Japanese Swords.* Osaka: Hoikusha, 1970.

Ono, Tadashi. *Nippon-to shokunin shokudan* [in Japanese]. Tokyo: Shuppan Kogei, 1973.

Robinson, B. W. *The Arts of the Japanese Sword.* London: Faber and Faber, 1961.

Sato, Kanzan. *The Japanese Sword.* Tokyo: Kodansha International, 1983.

Sherby, Oleg D., and Jeffrey Wadsworth. "Damascus Steels." *Scientific American* 252 (1985): 112–20.

Smith, Cyril Stanley. *A Search for Structure: Selected Essays in Science, Art, and History.* Cambridge, Mass.: MIT Press, 1981.

———. "A Metallographic Examination of Some Japanese Sword Blades." In *La tecnica di fabbricazione delle lame di acciaio presso gli antichi.* Milan: Centro per la Storia della Metallurgia A.I.M., 1957.

Tanimura, Hiromi. "Development of the Japanese Sword." *Journal of Metals* 32, no. 2 (February 1980): 63–73.

Yumoto, John M. *The Samurai Sword.* Tokyo: Charles E. Tuttle, 1958.

Index